Believing in You

Sharon C. Cooper

Amaris Publishing LLC

Believing In You

By
Sharon C. Cooper

Copyright © 2025 Sharon C. Cooper
Amaris Publishing LLC

All rights reserved. No part of this book may be used or reproduced in any manner without written permission except in the case of brief quotations embodied in critical articles and reviews. For permission, contact the author at www.sharoncooper.net

ISBN: 978-1-946172-57-0
Paperback

This story is a work of fiction. Names, characters, and incidents are either products of the author's imagination or are used fictitiously. Any resemblance to actual events, locales, organizations or persons, living or dead, is entirely coincidental.

Dedication

MsPrissy, you're a gift that keeps on giving! Love you!

Chapter One

"Nyla Elizabeth Priestly, if you don't come on, you're getting left!"

Nyla cringed at the sound of her sister's high pitch threat that traveled down the long hallway to her bedroom. Well, not exactly her bedroom, but Cree's guest room that Nyla had been using for the last few weeks.

Okay, maybe it had been months, but still, hearing her full name yelled like that reminded her of when they were kids. Their mother was good about putting them on blast, especially if she wanted to embarrass them in front of their friends.

But they weren't kids anymore, and Cree was not her mother, even if Nyla had to remind her of that on occasion. Cree, the second to the oldest of five kids, took her role of big sister seriously, and her bossiness had spilled over into their adult life. It didn't matter that Nyla was thirty-three, and Cree, who was three years older, still managed to make her feel like a child.

This morning, though, Nyla wasn't in the mood. She hadn't slept well thanks to thinking about her life. She was working two jobs and trying to save every penny so she could purchase Moody Days Jazz Club.

She was currently the manager there, but a few years ago, her boss, Gordon, told her that when he retired, he'd sell the business to her. Nyla had always wanted to be her own boss, and she loved the club. This was going to be the perfect opportunity for her, and she had started right after that conversation.

The problem was, he recently told her the asking price, and though it was a fair price, he planned to retire this spring. It was January. She only had a few months to finish stacking her dollars.

Grabbing her oversized bag from the foot of the bed, Nyla glanced around the bedroom and its Mediterranean style theme, making sure she wasn't leaving anything. Specifically, her extra clothes and shoes—as well as travel size toiletries—in case she spent the night at her parents' place.

Cree's guestroom wasn't huge, but what it lacked in size it made up for in elegance. Expensive furnishings and linens were highlighted by exposed beams, hardwood floors with a huge area rug in earthy tones, terra cotta ceramic nicknacks, and an ensuite. Her sister had always had expensive taste and insisted on the finer things in life, and Nyla was currently benefiting from that fact.

Jogging down the hallway, she needed to hurry if she didn't want to get left. She was bumming a ride with Cree who worked in the Loop. Downtown Chicago would get Nyla close to the temp job she had at an IT company.

"Finally," Cree grumbled when Nyla made it to the living room/dining room combination. The large, open floor plan also gave a view of the high-end kitchen. "Starting next week, if you want a ride to work, you'll need to be down here thirty minutes earlier. Otherwise, I'll already be gone. And what the heck are you wearing?"

Nyla stared down at her clothes as if she didn't remember what she was wearing. Her style was what she thought of as modern-day grunge. She smoothed her hand down her floor-length multi-color sweater that she had paired with black baggy pants and a multi-color, button-up shirt. She had topped the outfit off with her usual rings on every finger, silver bangles on her wrists, and her black, chunky, knee-high boots.

"I look perfectly fine," she said and grabbed her heavy coat from the closet. She'd been doing temp work at Telecom Solutions for a while now, and no one there complained about her style.

Her sister, an entertainment lawyer, always dressed to impress with her overpriced suits and equally expensive shoes, boots, and handbags. While Nyla was the opposite. Why spend every penny on clothes when you can find items just as nice at thrift shops and garage sales?

"Don't worry about how I look, sis, just focus on your own self," Nyla said. "I'm taking care of me."

Cree's eyebrows shot up, and she placed a hand on her narrow hip.

"Are you, though? You're bumming rides with me. You're living under my roof, sleeping in one of my beds, and eating my food. How are you taking care of yourself?"

"I don't eat your food!" Nyla snapped, then thought about the cereal and milk that she had finished off in the middle of the night. "I don't eat much of your food, and don't worry, I'll replace the cereal, milk, and those double-stuffed Oreos that we both demolished over the weekend. Now, are you happy? Can I go and grab my lunch from the refrigerator so we can go?"

Cree shook her head. "I love you, Lil Sis, but you're too old to be acting like some broke college student. I get that you're trying to save money, but you have to be smart. You need to rethink your priorities and grow up."

The moment the words were out of her sister's mouth, Nyla could see that she hadn't meant to say them out loud. Cree opened her mouth to probably apologize, but Nyla turned away and headed to the kitchen for the lunch she'd made last night.

Her insecurity about not being smart enough reared its ugly head. Normally, she was comfortable in her own skin and loved herself. She also knew she was just as intelligent as the next person, but still, this was an area in her life that sometimes made her doubt herself.

Unlike her three sisters who'd graduated from college, and her brother who'd served in the Marines, Nyla only had a high school education. She had learned early on that college wasn't for her. She was more artsy than her siblings, and formal education hadn't been her thing. So, over the years, she had only taken enough college courses to help her get the jobs she wanted. Such as the management position at the jazz club. She'd also gotten a certification in administrative support, which had been serving her well.

But when her last boyfriend told her he needed someone more his equal, then proceeded to dump her, her insecurity flared. And this morning, Cree wasn't helping. Yes, she had been nothing but supportive and patient over the past year, knowing why Nyla was saving her money. Yet sometimes she was insensitive.

Nyla's sacrifices were paying off. She was so close to reaching her financial goals. Yes, her sister was right about the lack of transportation, food, and penny pinching, but she didn't have to throw it in her face. Worse than that, though, it was the part about her needing to grow up that hit a nerve.

After grabbing her lunch bag, Nyla headed to the door and walked out of the apartment. She stomped to the elevator, fuming. How many times had people, specifically her family, said she needed to grow up? Or she was too trusting? Or she needed to go back to college and get her degree? Or she needed to stop living in la-la land?

Too many times to count, and she was sick of it. She was a grown ass woman doing the best she could to create a good life for herself. Maybe it was taking longer than planned, but she was getting there.

"Nyla, wait. I'm sorry. I was out of line," Cree said as she hurried after her.

They lived in a luxury apartment complex in Hyde Park, both loving the culturally diverse neighborhood. Whenever Nyla did move, she was going to miss the life of luxury the apartment building offered.

They entered the elevator, and Nyla stabbed a finger at the ground floor button.

"Nyla, I know how hard you've been working, and I want to see you realize all your dreams. But you've been on this quest for years. At some point, you're going to have to stop using all of us and start standing more on your own."

In "using all of us" she meant that she was going to have to stop couch surfing at their siblings' places. She also needed to stop bumming rides and showing up at their houses for breakfast, lunch, and sometimes dinner.

Though her sister's delivery could've been kinder, Cree was being herself. She always spoke her mind, even if it hurt to hear what she had to say.

"You're right," Nyla said reluctantly. "I need to take care of myself. If you can drop me off at the train station, I won't ask for a ride again. As for—"

"Nyla, it's not like I—"

"And if you can just give me one more month of free rent and board, I'll be on my way after that."

Cree huffed. "Of course you can stay with me. I'll always

support whatever you set out to do. It's just that you're squirreling away every penny to buy the club from your boss, but have you thought about living expenses? What are you going to live on if you buy the business?"

Nyla had been thinking about everything Cree said. Yes, there were some changes she needed to make, and she'd figure it all out. Right now, though, she needed to leave, or she was going to be late for work.

"As usual, *you're right*, but like I said, you don't have to worry about me." Nyla tried to keep the annoyance out of her voice but couldn't. "I can and will take care of myself, but thanks for all you've done. Have a good day. I'll get myself to work," she said, and seconds later, the elevator doors slid open.

Nyla walked out with her head held high and ignored Cree when her sister called after her. If she was going to grow up and stand on her own, might as well start now. Instead of heading to the garage where Cree parked, Nyla, with a smile on her face, made her way to the front entrance with a renewed confidence. She could get herself to work from now on.

But the moment she stepped outside, her smile faltered as a strong gust of wind pushed her sideways, almost knocking her over.

Good Lord. What the hell had she been thinking, trying to stand her ground when it was twenty degrees outside? She grumbled all the way to the $51^{st}/53^{rd}$ street station to catch the train.

Dammit, I hate adulting.

Chapter Two

Forty minutes later, Nyla's teeth were clattering as she rubbed her gloved hands together while entering the office building where Telecom Solutions was located. It didn't matter that she had layered her clothes and had on her warmest boots; she was cold down to her bones.

As she moved with a crowd of people heading to the bank of elevators, she rubbed her hands up and down her arms, trying to get her blood circulating again. She was sure it had frozen in her veins. The rest of her body hadn't fared much better.

By the time the elevators opened onto her floor, she could at least feel her fingers and toes. She was also able to say good morning to people without stuttering from being so cold. Telecom Solutions occupied the whole seventeenth floor.

Nyla headed down the hallway, past several offices, until she reached the area where the managers were housed. She supported three of them, but for the most part, they were all self-sufficient.

The moment Nyla approached her desk, the outside line was ringing. Technically, she had ten minutes before her shift started, but she set her bag down and picked up the phone.

"Good morning. Thank you for calling Telecom Solutions. How may I help you?"

After a slight hesitation, the caller said, "May I speak with Harrison Grant?"

"One minute, please," Nyla said and transferred the call to Harrison, knowing it would go straight to voicemail.

He normally met with his team first thing on Wednesday morning in the small conference room and usually didn't make it to his desk until nine-thirty. Which was good. It gave her a chance to get herself mentally together before she saw him. The man was hella fine, and even after being there a couple of months, her body still tingled with desire whenever she was near him.

As she shrugged out of her coat and hung it on the coat tree behind her desk, she thought about the erotic dreams she'd been having of him. Well, not just him, but the two of them together having sex on his desk, in the storage closet, and even in the women's bathroom. Her dreams were out of control and only left her frustrated and breathless whenever she came back to herself.

It didn't make sense that she was fantasizing and sometimes daydreaming about the man. *Why him?* Why did her temporary boss make her want to touch him all over and jump his bones? Sure, it had been awhile since she'd been with a man, but it hadn't been that damn long. And sure, he was handsome in a sexy, geek kind of way with an intelligence that was as attractive as the rest of him. However, he was uptight, standoffish, and a workaholic.

So not my type.

Even with those negatives, the sexual tension that vibed between her and Harrison Grant was hot enough to leave burn marks. It was a good thing that her assignment would soon be over. She didn't know how much longer she could pretend she wasn't seriously interested in him.

Then again, who was she kidding? The man was so far out of her league, there was no way he'd be interested in her. It didn't matter anyway. He seemed like the type to never step out of line. No way would he help her act out some of the fantasies.

Nyla snorted at the thought and shoved her bag into the bottom desk drawer. No sense in daydreaming about someone she could never...

The door behind her burst open, and she jumped, her hand flying to her chest. "What in the..."

Harrison.

"I told you to always get the caller's name and tell me before transferring them to my phone," he ground out, his chest heaving as if he was about to blow a gasket at any moment.

Nyla should be concerned, especially since he had never raised his voice at her, but all she could do was stare at him. The man was too gorgeous for his own good, and the fire in his eyes only made him look that much hotter.

Even his black, wire-rimmed glasses didn't detract from his handsomeness. Smooth deep-bronze skin, a thin mustache and goatee, and eyes that were so dark, they almost looked black, made up his perfect face. Then there was the black turtleneck he was wearing. It molded over his muscular upper body, and the black slacks had to be tailored specifically for him to look that good.

Yup. Too damn fine.

"Did you hear what I said?" he snapped, and that shook Nyla from her thoughts.

"I heard you," she said, though she wasn't positive that

she'd heard everything. Ignoring his rant and scowl, she said, "Good morning, Sunshine. Can I get you some coffee? Tea? Or do you need something stronger, like a shot of tequila, to calm you down?"

* * *

Stunned into silence, all Harrison could do was stare at the enticing woman who made him crazy. Not because she couldn't handle the admin work. No, she was wonderful in the position. His issues stemmed from the fact that he was attracted to the unflappable beauty.

Not only was she beautiful in an understated way, but she was the most easygoing person he'd ever met. Nothing phased her. Not even him—storming out of his office and verbally attacking her like an idiot—but phone calls from certain people tended to have that effect on him.

Huffing out a breath, Harrison stuffed his hands into the front pockets of his black pants and finally *really* looked at Nyla. Mischief glimmered in her eyes, and a grin spread across her lips. Her enticing, red, plump lips that he wanted to kiss more than he wanted to do anything else.

Apparently, Nyla Priestly was the cure for all things that ailed him because the phone call was all but forgotten, and his lips twitched as he tried to fight a smile.

"I think I need more than a shot of liquor this morning," he finally said, remembering how she'd greeted him. "So if you have tequila, just hand over the whole bottle."

Her mouth dropped open, and her eyes grew wide at his words. Hell, he was surprised too. He didn't crack jokes. He barely talked to anyone, but there was something about this woman who brought out a side of him that he didn't even recognize himself.

Laughing, she folded her arms across her chest and leaned a hip against the desk. "Well, well, well. Who knew you had a sense of humor? And I've been working here for months, and I can't remember you ever smiling. At least not the way you're currently smiling, where the smile actually makes it to your eyes. Who are you, and what have you done with the grumpy Mr. Harrison Grant?"

On that, Harrison couldn't help but laugh. He shook his head and took a few steps back. He didn't trust himself to be too close to this woman because he might do something else that was uncharacteristic of him. Something like pull her into his arms, hold her close, and finally find out what she tasted like.

Nope, he couldn't risk it.

Thoughts of what it would be like to kiss Nyla had dominated his mind lately but kissing her was forbidden. Hell, even touching her wasn't a good idea. At least as far as he was concerned. The company didn't have a no fraternizing policy, but no way would Harrison get involved with an employee. Not even a temporary one.

Yeah, he needed to shut down this attraction toward her. Besides, he didn't do relationships, and Nyla came across as the settling down type. Something he never planned to do. *Ever.*

When the desk phone rang, she answered it, and it was the perfect opportunity for Harrison to return to his office and close the door. Instead, his gaze took in her unique appearance. He didn't know what the oversize clothing style was called, but it looked good on her. Hell, everything looked good on her. Though most days she wore outfits that hid her body, he'd had the pleasure of seeing her in formal wear at their holiday party last month. The little black dress had shown off all her curves. Including full breasts, a narrow waist, and legs that went on for days, even though she couldn't have been more than 5'5".

Today though, she wasn't showing any skin, but her lovely face was enough. Her dark, curly hair was cut in a short feminine style, and he wondered if the curls were as soft as they looked. Her eye makeup was bold, with dark eyeliner and long lashes that didn't look fake. Then there was the deep-red lipstick she was wearing that made her kissable lips all the more tempting. If only...

"Hold for a minute, please. I'll see if he's available," Nyla said, her words snatching him out of his thoughts. "Someone named Warren from Ludlum's Marketing wants to speak with you. Are you available?"

"Yes, give me a minute, then patch him through," Harrison said as he walked away, but then he stopped and turned back to Nyla. "I'm sorry for the way I acted a few minutes ago. I had no right charging out here talking to you like that. It won't happen again."

Nyla shrugged his apology off. "No worries, but I take it you don't need that tequila anymore?"

Harrison chuckled. "Nah, I'm good, but thanks for the offer."

"You're welcome, and since we're on the subject, who's the person who makes you contemplate having tequila first thing in the morning? I'm only asking because I can do a better job screening the calls. That way, instead of bothering you when the person calls, I can tell them you're not available. Then you won't be forced to do your imitation of a grizzly bear again."

Damn. Had he really behaved that badly? Probably, and he could only imagine how he'd sounded.

He inhaled deeply and released the breath slowly. "Let's just say I'd rather talk to the devil himself than talk to my mother."

Harrison ignored the way Nyla sputtered, clearly trying to

come up with something to say. He didn't give her a chance to respond as he returned to his office.

Maybe he should've told her to add his ex-fiancée to that short list. His feelings for both women were the same. Their betrayals might've happened years ago, but he still would rather have a conversation with Satan than either of them.

Chapter Three

I'd rather talk to the devil himself than talk to my mother.

Hours later, Nyla was still thinking about Harrison's words. The admission didn't fit the man she knew. Not that she knew him well, but despite his grumpiness, he was a really nice guy.

That wasn't just her opinion, but it was also the opinion of the people who worked for and with him. Harrison wasn't the most social supervisor, but he cared about his staff, and it showed in the things he did for them—like spring for lunch once a week. Or like when Melody's husband had gotten sick at work, and she'd needed a ride to get to him. Harrison didn't think twice about taking her to him.

The list of his kind deeds went on and on. So, hearing him speak of his mother that way had caught Nyla off guard. She couldn't imagine feeling that way about her mother, who she talked to regularly. No, they got along great, as did everyone in their family. They were a lively bunch, and though they didn't always agree with one another, family always came first with them.

But what had the woman done to Harrison to make him despise her? There had to be a story there, and Nyla was nosy enough to want to know.

"It's none of my business," she mumbled as she locked the desk drawer and started for the storage room. *None of my business at all.*

"Nyla!"

She had barely taken a few steps when she saw Wendy, one of the software developers, rushing toward her. Nyla leaned against her desk.

"I'm glad I caught you. I have something for you," said the woman, who was at least ten years older than Nyla.

"For me?"

"Yes, for you." Wendy brushed long, dark hair from her face as she dug through her messenger bag. "I wanted to thank you for your help yesterday, and I know how much you love these sweet treats. Which is why I picked one up for you. Hopefully, it's not too squished."

Nyla recognized the bag and grinned. If it was what she thought it was, she didn't care if it was a crumbly mess. "Tell me this is a white chocolate and macadamia nut cookie."

"It is!" Wendy said on a laugh. "That's just my way of saying thanks for testing out that app yesterday."

"Are you kidding? That was fun," Nyla said, pinching off a piece of the cookie and deciding that she'd save the rest for later. "It amazes me the type of work you guys do around here. I can't wait until that game hits the App Store. I don't play many games on my phone, but that's one I'm looking forward to."

"Thanks. We've been working on it for awhile, and it's getting closer to being done, but there are still a few bugs to work out."

They talked a few minutes about a couple of other projects,

and Nyla was in awe at how software developers came up with some of their ideas. Wendy was highly educated and talked with such passion when discussing her work.

Nyla wondered if that's how she sounded when she talked about her music and Moody Days. She played a few instruments, but the one she loved most was the piano, and she'd even written some music. Though they might never be heard out in the world, she could talk about them, and some of her musical adaptations of popular songs, all day.

As for Moody Days, that place was her heart, even though she didn't own it yet. The way she could go on and on about what they were doing there, and the plans she had for the future, people were probably sick of hearing about the place. The club felt like home whenever she stepped through the doors, which was why she had to do whatever she could to purchase the business.

Those were her thoughts after she finished talking to Wendy and entered the storage room. She was going to spend a few minutes unpacking boxes of supplies that had been dropped off earlier. Thankfully, she had caught the delivery guy before he left everything in the receptionist area. He'd been kind enough to put the large boxes just inside the storage room.

Digging into her pants pocket, Nyla pulled out her earbuds. Instead of putting both into her ears, she only used one of them so she could hear the phone if it rang. A few minutes later, she was humming along to Jill Scott's "Getting in the Way."

Nyla made quick work of unpacking most of the boxes as she grooved to the music. Once she realized she was going to run out of room on the lower shelves, she started doing some rearranging. Hopefully, no one would mind, but even if they did, she wouldn't be there much longer.

The administrative assistant she was filling in for was due back in a few days, and Nyla was going to miss everyone at Telecom Solutions. Normally, her job assignments were rarely more than a week or two, which she preferred. But being at Telecom longer than usual had been great. Everyone had been so welcoming from day one, and there were some who she felt like she'd known all her life.

It was going to be hard to leave, and if she'd been looking for a full-time position, she would see if they were hiring, but she wasn't. She had only decided to do temp work as a side hustle to help build her savings a bit quicker.

Nyla glanced at the last two boxes, one full of various computer hardware and the other containing a few routers.

Now, where to put this stuff? she thought as she glanced around the small room that was bigger than an average supply closet. She moved a box that was labeled cords, planning to put it on a higher shelf, but stopped when dust flew into her face.

"Ugh," she groaned and coughed a few times while waving her hand back and forth to clear the air. Maybe she should be dusting while reorganizing.

After moving another box to the floor, she continued unpacking her last two boxes. Then she grabbed the folding ladder that was in the corner and opened it near where she was going to store the cords.

"*I'm not your superwoman,*" Nyla sang along with Karyn White, whose song "Superwoman" was blaring in her ear.

She made two trips up the ladder, and on the way back down the second time, she realized the desk phone was ringing. She'd been so caught up in singing and moving items around on the top shelf, Nyla wasn't sure how long it had been ringing.

She hurried down the steps, but the tail of her sweater got caught on the edge of one of the rungs, causing her to stumble and the ladder to sway.

Her heart lodged in her throat. "Oh, crap!"

"What the hell are you doing?" Harrison barked.

Nyla shrieked in surprise at his outburst and tried to grip the top of the ladder just as it started tilting. She lost her grip, and the floor rushed up to meet her, but her momentum suddenly stopped. Strong hands slid around her waist and beneath her knees. Next thing she knew, she was holding on tightly around Harrison's neck as he cradled her against his hard, powerful body. And dammit if she didn't like this position.

Chest heaving and breaths coming in short spurts, Nyla stared wide-eyed into his handsome face that was only inches from hers. He was so damn close. *Too* damn close. Her mouth was only inches from his, and it was taking all her self-control not to lean forward and cover his juicy lips with hers.

But she couldn't move. It was as if they were both frozen in place, neither speaking a word as their eyes searched each other's.

The man was even more beautiful up close, and if that weren't enough, he smelled magnificent. His clean, fresh, alluring scent reached her nostrils, and Nyla breathed in deeply and tried not to moan.

Goodness.

Would it be too weird to bury her nose against his neck and sniff him? Probably. Or maybe she could just lay her head on his shoulder and bask in his scent and his strength. Yeah, she could stay in this position forever.

While her thoughts went wild, she realized Harrison still hadn't spoken, not that she was surprised. He was a man of few words, but what did surprise her was that he was still holding her against his incredible body. He acted as if she weighed nothing.

No way was she going to break the spell that he was clearly

under. Not when she was given the opportunity to feel his hard, muscular chest against hers. Nah, they could stay like this until the...

"Oh, there you are. I..." someone's voice sounded from the open door, then trailed off. "Um...never mind. This can wait. Carry on," the person said in a rush, and Nyla heard their footsteps take them away.

And just like that, the spell was broken. Harrison quickly set her on her feet, then took a giant step away from her. Nyla immediately felt the loss, but what had she expected? That he was going to stand there for the rest of the day with her in his arms?

"Thanks for the assist," she said, unsure of what else to say to make this moment less awkward.

Harrison only grunted and headed for the door while rubbing his hand over his low haircut. "Stay off the damn ladder," were his parting words as he practically ran from the room.

Nyla released a long breath. Someone really needed to snap that man out of his grumpy funk. Too bad it wouldn't be her since she'd only be there a few more days.

Then again, it would probably take an act of God to straighten the guy out.

***

What the actual hell? Harrison thought when he entered his office and slammed the door behind him. He rubbed the back of his neck as he stormed to his desk.

Nyla was getting to him.

The eccentric woman had done in two months what most women hadn't been able to do in years. She'd gotten around his defenses. Harrison couldn't remember the last time he'd wanted to kiss a woman as bad as he'd wanted to kiss Nyla. Which was saying a lot. His ex-fiancée had done such a number on him, he'd barely looked at another woman, and he'd wanted to keep it that way.

Then Nyla, with her quick wit, perky everything, and a soft curvy body that felt perfect in his arms. Every nerve within him had come alive, and he hadn't wanted to put her down. Had they not been interrupted, Harrison was sure he would've kissed her, and that would've been a huge mistake.

Damn the woman for making him want her.

Two more days. In two days, his administrative assistant would be back, and everything could go back to normal.

Just two more days.

Chapter Four

Later that night, Nyla leaned against the bar and glanced around Moody Days Jazz Club, feeling proud of herself. As the manager, she'd been trying to come up with ways of generating more income into the business. Not only that, but she also wanted to double the number of customers they averaged every night, and she was making progress.

Now all she had to do was double her savings in the next few months, and then the club would be hers. Well, maybe not double, but she needed a little more money.

No pressure.

Not only was she concerned about the money, doubts of whether she could actually run a business on her own had been creeping in lately. Sure, she was a great manager, but when she became the owner, all the responsibilities, including the financials, would be on her.

Which was why she was trying to prove to herself that she could make her dream come true. She could be a successful business owner even if she only had a high school education.

Believing in You

I can do this. I can make the club a success.

Smooth jazz flowed from the stage where a trio played a familiar song, and Nyla glanced around. Most of the after-work crowd appeared to be enjoying the music, while other customers talked amongst themselves in small groups.

The place wasn't huge, but it was large enough to hold events, which was something Nyla had started doing more often. Like tonight. Tonight, Wednesday, was their first open mic night, and so far, it was a success. Thanks to advertising around the neighborhood and on social media, the response had been amazing. So much so, they'd had to limit the number of performers. She now had a waiting list for the following two Wednesdays.

Thursdays were lady's night, and Friday and Saturdays were the days they hired entertainment—local groups—to perform. Despite that expense, over the last three months, she had increased the jazz club's profits by twenty percent.

This is good, she thought, but immediately, her mind shifted to her own finances. She didn't know how or when, but she was determined to get the rest of the money needed. She had to.

"Are you going to stand there staring out into space all night, or are you going to actually do some work?"

Nyla smiled at her best friend Jamie's words and turned to face him. "It looks like you have things under control," she said just loud enough to be heard over the music.

"Of course I do," Jamie said, a bit of arrogance in his tone as he filled two drink orders at the same time. He made it look so easy. Once done, he set them on the tray, and the server carried them away. He turned back to Nyla. "What's on your mind tonight?"

Considering it was mid-January and freezing outside, Jamie sported a T-shirt that stretched across his wide chest and hugged his muscular pecks. He had played football in college over ten years ago, and he still managed to stay in tip-top shape.

Nyla knew for a fact that the man's good looks and charming ways were the reason they attracted so many women into the club. He was ruggedly handsome, with shoulder-length dreadlocks that added to his masculine appeal.

They first met ten years ago when her mother was going through her match-making phase and thought it a good idea to set them up on a blind date. The date didn't go well, but a great friendship came out of it, and they'd been besties ever since.

"S*ooo*, what's on your mind?" Jamie asked again, then leaned slightly across the bar, bringing them closer. "Let me guess. You're still trying to figure out how you can buy the club. I know it's been weighing heavily on you. Maybe you can just —"

"You don't think I can do it, do you?" she snapped, unable to stop the words from flying out of her mouth. No one thought she could do it, and if she was honest, there were moments she feared they might be right. "I expect doubt from my family, but you? You know how much this means to me."

"Nyla."

"No, I have been saving, sacrificing, and putting all my energy into making this a place to call my own. I don't care what anyone says, even if I only have a high school diploma, I'm smart enough to run a business, dammit!" she spat as emotion swirled inside of her. "I've been doing it for years, and I've been doing a damn good job. The numbers speak for themselves."

Breathing hard, she glared at him as he stared at her with his left eyebrow lifted questioningly. When he didn't respond, she huffed out a breath.

Crap. She'd overreacted. What was wrong with her? Why was she suddenly letting doubts plague her mind? Jamie nor her family could say anything as it related to buying the club without her snapping on them.

"Are you done?" he asked, and she felt like a fool.

Jamie was her biggest supporter, and he never talked about her lack of education. Actually, neither had her family. It was just that she felt inferior to all of them, including Jamie. Everyone had a college degree except for her.

Nyla had had plenty of opportunities to continue her education, but college had been too confining. She was a creative, a free spirit, artsy type woman who typically did her own thing her own way.

Still, every now and then, she wished she would've done more than just take a couple of college courses. And the main reason she'd taken a small business management class, as well as accounting for beginners, was because Gordon, the owner of Moody Days, insisted she do that before giving her the manager position.

Nyla had been working at the jazz club in some capacity since graduating from high school. She had wanted to be a professional pianist when she grew up. Though she was good after years of lessons, there were so many people better than her. So instead of continuing her education, she hung around the club and musicians.

"I'm sorry," she finally said, feeling silly for being so sensitive, and she knew it stemmed from the conversation with Cree earlier that day. Cree might've been supportive of her choices, but she still thought Nyla was wasting her talents hanging out in the club. At least that's how she made her feel sometimes.

"What I was going to say is maybe you can ask Gordon to give you more time to get the funds together."

She could, but he'd been adamant that this spring he'd be retiring. Her parents had offered to loan her the rest of the money, but Nyla didn't want their financial help. Nor did she want her siblings to chip in. If they did, they'd expect to have a say in how she ran the business, and that's not what she wanted.

"Remember that guy I wanted you to meet?" Jamie asked, abruptly changing the subject. "The one you said 'no' to before I could even list his qualities?"

Nyla shook her head. "Jamie, you're getting as bad as my mother. I'm not going on a blind date. I don't care if he is a good friend of yours or how awesome he is. I'm not interested. Besides, I have enough going on. I don't need to add a man to the mix."

"Well, you're going to meet him anyway. I think if you get to know him, you'll understand why I think you two are perfect for each other." He glanced behind her. "And he's right on time."

Nyla looked over her shoulder, and it was as if all the air was sucked out of the room. "You gotta be kidding me."

Harrison Grant strolled in.

Heat flooded Nyla's body, and she swallowed hard as her heart rate amped up. Wiping her suddenly damp palms down the front of her pants, she tried to look away. No sense of getting caught staring, but she couldn't help it. He looked larger than life as he entered.

He was wearing a wool cap pulled low on his forehead and a scarf around his neck. The tan peacoat looked stylish and expensive, and like everything he wore, the outerwear didn't hide his muscular body.

Detailed memories of how good it felt to be cradled in his strong arms rushed to the forefront of her mind. The intensity with which he'd looked at her. His scent. His mouth. All of it had every cell in her body sparking to attention. While desire ping-ponged within her and had her squeezing her thighs together.

This is not good.

Nyla swallowed hard as Harrison's long, sexy gait carried him farther into the building, but a man he was about to walk past stopped him. When they shook hands and started talking, Nyla released a long breath that she hadn't realized she'd been holding.

Get it together, woman.

Wait.

She turned back to Jamie who was grinning.

"By the way you were licking your lips, I'd say I chose well for you."

"He's my boss," she whisper shouted, and Jamie frowned. "He's the guy I report to at my temp job." Jamie had no way of knowing that since she rarely discussed her temp jobs with him.

"Get the heck out of here," he said, and then he burst out laughing. "Fate. It's gotta be fate, and the way you were just drooling over him—"

"I wasn't drooling," she grumbled under her breath. "I was just surprised." She took another peek over her shoulder, and Harrison was still talking to the other guy. "Quick. What's Harrison's story? He seems like a nice guy, but—"

"He's cool," Jamie interrupted as he wiped down the bar. "One of the best men I know. Otherwise, I wouldn't be trying to hook you two up. I'm not sure how he is at work, but he's funny, dependable, and there'd been a time when he'd do anything for anybody. Unfortunately, a few years ago..."

When his voice trailed off, and he glanced away, Nyla followed his gaze that landed on Harrison.

"What happened a few years ago?" she asked.

After a slight hesitation, Jamie huffed. "Let's just say he's been through some things. Things that shook him to the point of not trusting people anymore, but I think you can help him with that. You're just what he needs. You interested?"

"Nope, just curious," Nyla lied, her words spilling out a little too quickly.

She was interested, but she was serious when she said she didn't have time for a relationship. Especially a relationship with someone with baggage, and Harrison came with a lot of it.

She knew all about trust issues and bad relationships. Her ex, John, had seen to that. One minute, she thought he was a great guy who really cared about her. The next, he'd made her feel like the lowest form of human life when he told her he was no longer interested in her. He'd wanted someone more of his equal.

Nyla took that to mean he wanted someone who worked in corporate America like he did. Or someone who was well educated, smart, and business savvy. Whatever he'd been looking for, clearly, she hadn't been it. But he'd found it a few weeks later. Nyla had run into him and a mystery woman at the theater when she and one of her sisters had gone to see Wicked. The couple looked extremely cozy, and she had a feeling they'd been seeing each other for a while.

Nyla stood straighter when Harrison headed toward the bar, and she noticed the moment he spotted her. He slowed, narrowed his beautiful, almond-shaped eyes, and then his gaze bounced between her and Jamie.

Behind her, Jamie was chuckling. "This is too funny," he said.

"This is not funny at all," Nyla deadpanned.

"Nyla? What are you doing here?" Harrison asked when he made it to the bar.

"I'm the manager of Moody Days," she said.

"Funny thing," Jamie said, giving his friend a fist bump, "Nyla is the woman I've been trying to get you to meet." Jamie glanced at her. "I don't know who's more stubborn, you or him.

I received the same brush off from both of you, and one thing is clear—you two like each other."

Nyla rolled her eyes at her friend. Maybe she should've listened when he'd said he had someone he wanted her to meet. Then she would've known it was Harrison and could've said, *no thanks*. But at that time, all she could think about was how often her mother tried to play matchmaker for her and her siblings. It was getting old.

"Manager?" Harrison said, ignoring Jamie as he glanced around the club before returning his attention to Nyla. "I didn't realize you had another job."

"Yeah, the temp jobs are my side hustle," she said absently, distracted by the way he was shrugging out of his overcoat.

He was still wearing what he'd worn to work earlier, but somehow his shoulders seemed broader. His chest wider. And his flat abs were more defined despite the dark fabric of his turtleneck.

Gawd, this man!

He was a tech guru. He was supposed to look geeky, bookish, and intelligent. Not sexy and sophisticated.

And another thought pinged in her mind. He was the opposite of her. Probably in every way possible, and she needed to squash whatever fascination this was between them. Besides being opposites, anyone could look at them and know Harrison was *way* out of her league.

"It's a small world," Jamie said, reminding Nyla that he was still standing there.

He set a beer bottle in front of Harrison just as he sat at the bar. "I'm glad you guys have already met. Now you can get to know each other better."

Harrison didn't respond as he sipped his beer. Maybe he was thinking what she was thinking—them together was a bad idea. Not just because they worked together, though, that would change in a few days. Even if it was clear there was an attraction between them, they'd never make it as a couple. Yes, he was intelligent, kindhearted, and he had a body that her hands and mouth yearned to explore. But he was also grumpy, standoffish, and he didn't smile enough.

What she didn't know was if he could kiss. Or if he wore boxers or briefs. Or what his favorite sexual position was, and yeah, at one time or another she'd wondered. She'd always been curious by nature, and Harrison ignited her curiosity to the ninth degree.

"Nyla?"

Her head jerked to Jamie who looked as if he'd called her name more than once. "Yeah?"

"Terry is trying to get your attention," he said, nodding his head toward the stairs that led to the stage. Terry was a new hire who was currently helping with open mic night.

"Ah, I'd better go see what's up."

Nyla started to walk away but stopped and placed her hand on Harrison's forearm. He stared at her hand before meeting her eyes.

"Don't leave before I get back," she said, knowing what she was thinking was probably a bad idea. But it wouldn't be her first one and probably not her last one.

Without waiting for a response, she strolled away, and a grin kicked up the corners of her lips. She wasn't looking for anything serious, but that didn't mean they couldn't explore whatever was vibing between them.

She'd been sacrificing a lot lately. She needed a little fun in her life, and maybe Harrison could help her out with that. At least physically.

Chapter Five

Harrison tried, but he couldn't stop himself from watching Nyla stroll away. Her sexy walk grabbed his attention every time. He wanted more than anything to pull her back, have her sit on his lap, and ravish her gorgeous mouth.

Which was insane.

He couldn't remember the last time he'd had those types of thoughts about a woman, but Nyla was different. From day one, Harrison had been drawn to her. So much so it kind of freaked him out. They didn't know each other well, but at work, he was so comfortable around her that it felt as if they'd known each other forever.

Nyla had that effect on him. The more time he spent in her presence, the more time he wanted to be near her. She was slowly pulling him from behind the protective wall that he'd erected around himself.

"Those are two of her sisters," Jamie said of the women who'd just walked up to Nyla and hugged her. He wasn't close enough to see if there was a family resemblance, but it was nice to see they at least got along.

Harrison once had a relationship like that with his family, but one fateful night changed that and everything else in his life. He'd been shattered by betrayal. He didn't communicate with most of his relatives, but he at least talked to his sister on occasion.

"I'm glad you came in tonight," Jamie said. "I need to leave before closing, but I don't want to abandon Nyla to close alone. Can you stick around and lock up with her?"

Harrison narrowed his eyes at his long-time friend. They'd grown up together but lost touch after graduating from college. He had run into Jamie a few years ago at a time when he needed a friend.

"I know what you're trying to do, and it's not going to work," Harrison said. "Matchmaking doesn't suit you, and you already know I'm damaged goods. Nyla deserves a man who can be everything she needs. Someone who can be emotionally present. I can't be that man."

He wished he could be that for Nyla because the woman stirred a longing in him that he hadn't felt in ages, if ever. Yes, he wanted to feel again. He wanted to start living again, and that included dating.

But...

"It's clear you're both interested in the other," Jamie said.

"That may be, but nothing could ever come of us." The words felt bitter on Harrison's tongue, but they were true.

"Even if she has expressed a serious interest in you?"

Harrison released a long sigh. It was nice to know he wasn't alone in his feelings. How many times had he dreamed about what it would be like to hold her in his arms and kiss her tempting lips? Which was why he'd been paralyzed earlier when she'd landed in his arms. He'd wanted to devour her mouth.

Even before that moment, he had thought about her more than he cared to admit. Unfortunately, he wasn't ready to open his heart to anyone. Not now, maybe not ever.

Still, she was beautiful inside and out, and he wanted to know everything about her—likes, dislikes, everything.

"It's time, Harrison," Jamie said. "You gotta let the past go and put yourself back out there again."

"I am," Harrison growled. "I'm here, aren't I?"

He'd once been outgoing and personable, but now, outside of going to work every day and maybe going to the grocery store, he had turned into a hermit.

Jamie nodded. "I'll admit, it is good seeing you, but what about dating? When was the last time you took a woman out to dinner or a movie?"

Harrison didn't respond. He didn't need to. Jamie already knew the answer. Had it not been for his friend's prodding, Harrison wouldn't be there.

After the drama that was his life, the last thing he'd wanted was to be out in public. It had been a few years since he'd been hounded by the media, but it had left an impression. Not a good one. Thanks to an invasion of privacy, a ton of embellishment, and total lack of human decency from the media, Harrison had disconnected from the world.

People sucked!

All those holier-than-though, self-righteous folks who sat at home or behind closed doors judging someone else's life. He hadn't even committed the crime he'd been accused of. Yet, people crucified him.

Harrison ran his hands down his face and breathed in. This was so not what he wanted to be thinking about tonight. There were some good people in the world, and he hated to lump everyone into one basket. It wasn't fair, especially after there'd been a handful of people back then who stood by him.

"Nyla would be good for you. Not only is she nice looking, but she's also fun, funny, and thoughtful. She's nothing like your ex-fiancée. She's someone who will be there for you no matter the situation."

Harrison believed him, but...

"You can't keep living like this, man," Jamie said.

There was no one sitting on the stool next to Harrison, which was good. His past wasn't something to discuss in public, but clearly that wasn't stopping Jamie even if he was keeping his voice low.

"What happened to you was beyond messed up. Unthinkable, even, but you can't let it continue holding you captive. You deserve some happiness."

Harrison nodded. Deep down, he wanted his life back, but it was hard to trust anyone. Even someone as sweet as Nyla.

"I know you, and I know you're feeling her. I saw it in your eyes the moment you saw her tonight."

"Jamie let's not do this," Harrison mumbled, then finished off his beer. "A lot has happened, and I'm not the same person."

Jamie opened another beer bottle and slid it to him. Two was his limit.

"I know what type of person you are, and I wouldn't push you toward Nyla if I didn't know you two would be good for each other."

Harrison didn't get a chance to ask Jamie to back off. A server approached Jamie to fill an order, giving Harrison the reprieve he needed. Yet, he couldn't help thinking about what it would be like to spend time with Nyla.

Later that evening, Nyla continued to impress Harrison. She was a jack of all trades and was currently behind the bar making drinks.

Believing in You

"Is there anything you *can't* do?" he asked after she served the last drink of the night. There were still a few people hanging out, but the club would be closing soon.

Nyla released an unladylike snort, then quickly slapped her hand over her mouth.

"Sorry," she laughed. "Your question surprised me since there are a ton of things I can't do. However, as manager, I had to learn every aspect of running this place. Some things I do better than others." She lifted the glass that she was rinsing. "Bartending just happens to be something I'm good at. Actually, it's probably the easiest job here."

From where Harrison was sitting, nothing about running the club appeared easy, but she seemed to enjoy it.

"You know, I appreciate you sticking around, but if you need to leave, it's totally fine. I've locked up alone before, and I hate that Jamie roped you into staying."

"I don't feel roped in at all. Besides, it's not a good idea for you to lock up alone. I'm glad to help. Just let me know what you need me to do to assist."

He might've griped at first when Jamie asked, only because he knew his friend was trying to push them together. He understood where Jamie was coming from, especially since he thought Harrison was wound too tight and needed to loosen up.

Maybe if he spent a little time with Nyla outside of work, she'd rub off on him. Hell, maybe she'd rub off on him in other ways too. Or maybe she could just rub all over him and...

Whoa. He needed to stop that train of thought. Hadn't he just admitted to not being good for her? That he wasn't good for anyone right now?

He needed to remember that because Nyla came across as a forever type of woman.

For the next hour, he helped wipe down tables, clean the bathrooms, and a host of other things. It was good she'd kept him busy. Otherwise, he probably would've spent the whole time staring at her and wondering what it would be like to kiss her.

"Whew!" Nyla said and leaned across the bar, then lifted her head and looked at him.

Harrison's dick stirred at the way her pretty eyes glimmered. His heart and mind might not be ready to start dating again, but his body was more than ready. He wanted Nyla even if it was a bad idea.

"Thank you for helping me," she said. "Normally, the tidying up goes faster, but we were short a server tonight and it showed. Things had gotten a little more backed up than I realized. I owe you."

Harrison shook his head. "You don't owe me anything. I'm glad I was able to help. So, is that it? Is there anything else you need to do before leaving?"

"Nope, that's it. Let's get out of here."

She disappeared to the back, then returned with her coat, scarf, and huge handbag. She set everything down on a table and started to slip into her heavy coat, but Harrison reached for it.

"Let me," he said, and held it open for her.

His heart squeezed when she looked up at him and flashed him a sexy smile. "Thank you." She slid her arms into the sleeves, then turned to him.

In that moment, staring into her eyes, something came over him, and Harrison gently tugged on the front of her coat and pulled her close.

Eyes as wide as saucers stared at him as he gently cupped her face between his hands and brushed her cheeks with the pad of his thumb. Her skin was as soft as he imagined it would be, and his heart squeezed as she searched his eyes.

So many emotions swirled inside of him—desire, affection,

joy, longing, and a desperate yearning to kiss her. What he was experiencing in this moment was more powerful than anything he'd felt in a long time.

Question was, should he act on what he wanted more than anything?

Nyla's gaze bounced between his eyes and his mouth. She wanted what he wanted. So instead of debating with himself, Harrison lowered his head and covered her lips with his. And in that moment, kissing her felt like coming home.

Chapter Six

I'm kissing Harrison.
  No, that's not right. Harrison is kissing me!
  Wait. No. We're kissing each other.
Holy crap!

Nyla's heart tripped over itself and was beating double time as Harrison slid his arm around her waist and pulled her even closer, deepening their connection. She was snug against his chest. At least as snug as their coats would allow, and he kissed her with so much passion, she moaned.

It wasn't just any kiss. It was one of those toe-curling, blow-your-mind, I-only-want-you, type of kisses. And she was totally here for it.

His lips, soft and commanding yet gentle, as well as his kissing ability, was everything she imagined. She moved her hands from his waist and slid them up his torso, then fisted the front of his coat within her grasp. A power surge of energy charged through her as their tongues continued tangling, and her body hummed with need.

She hadn't been kissed in so long, she hadn't realized how

much she missed the connection, the closeness, the tenderness. She couldn't ever remember being kissed so thoroughly, especially not by John, her ex.

But Harrison?

Nyla could already tell he was in a league of his own when it came to knowing how to treat a woman. If he was as thorough in other areas as he was in kissing, she wanted to experience each one.

"Harrison," she moaned against his lips. "I..."

Harrison froze for a split second before tearing his mouth from hers, and Nyla could've kicked herself. She didn't even know what she was going to say to him, but if she would've kept her big mouth shut, she could still be enjoying their lip-lock.

Why'd he have to stop? What had freaked him out? Because he was definitely freaked out if the horrified expression on his handsome face was any indication.

"I'm sorry," he hurried to say. "I—I..."

"I'm not," Nyla interrupted.

It was as if she could still feel Harrison's mouth on hers as she touched her lips with her fingers.

Yeah, no, she wasn't sorry. At. All.

Silence fell between them. While she studied him, he studied his stylishly black leather boots while shaking his head.

He huffed out a breath before looking at her. "I was out of line. I wish I could say it won't happen again, but... You're so damn irresistible. I couldn't help myself."

Nyla grinned, and then she burst out laughing because of how serious he looked. By their interactions and conversations over the last couple of months at work, she knew Harrison wasn't shy. Yet, there was an innocence about his current behavior that didn't fit.

The man was such a contradiction. He was a contrast of tall, sexy, take charge, and well put together man in one instance. Then the next, he was aloof, unsure, and almost skittish. It was as if he wanted to let himself go and live a little, but something was holding him back.

"I liked it, and I'm looking forward to the next time we do it," she said. Attempting to lighten the moment, she moved forward and gave him a quick kiss on the cheek. He momentarily stiffened but then relaxed.

Ready to go home, Nyla went back to her locking up routine. She started shutting off lights, and Harrison eventually followed her to the back hallway. He stood by the exit while she reached into the utility closet and turned on the alarm.

Once they made it outside, the bitterly cold wind whipped around her and sent a chill through her body. It had reached thirty-eight degrees earlier, but now, it had to be in the teens.

"Where's your car?" Harrison asked, glancing around the back of the building. There were two empty parking spaces against the building, as well as a dumpster close to the alley.

"I sold it last year," she said and slung the strap of her bag onto her shoulders before sliding her hands into her fur-lined gloves.

She'd had to make sacrifices, including going without a car. Thankfully, Chicago had great public transportation that got her everywhere she wanted to go. At least for the most part. Occasionally, she did rideshare but not often because of the cost.

Harrison frowned. "How do you get to and from work?"

"The train or sometimes the bus."

She glanced at her watch. If she hustled, she'd make it in time to catch the next train home.

"Well, thanks for sticking around, Harrison. I appreciate it. The next time you come in, food and drinks are on me. See you in the morning."

Harrison fell into step beside her. "I can't let you catch the train this time of night. I'll take you home. I'm parked around the corner."

Nyla smiled at him. "It'll be fine. I do it all the time."

"Not tonight," he said, and the finality in his deep baritone left no room for argument.

"But Harrison, I don't live around here. I'm in Hyde Park, and I think I remember you mentioning you live in Lincoln Park. I can't ask you to go out of your way like that. I appreciate you helping me lock up, but you've done enough."

The club, located in Bucktown, was not far from where he lived. But if he drove her home, that was at least a thirty-minute ride each way.

"It's not a problem, Nyla. Besides, it'll make me feel better knowing you were safe. This way," he said, nodding down the street to his left.

She shivered and pulled the hood of her coat over her head to help block out the wind. A ride in the car this time of night would be better than hopping on the train, especially considering how much the temperature had dropped.

"Fine, as long as you know it's not necessary."

He didn't respond, and a few minutes later, he stopped next to a new Ford Explorer. She pictured him as more of a luxury car type of guy, but winters in Chicago could be brutal, especially when it snowed. An SUV was definitely a better choice.

He opened the passenger side door and helped her into the vehicle before he climbed into the driver's seat. After giving him her address, she settled in for the ride.

Small talk flowed between them. Nothing too heavy, despite Nyla wanting to ask him some personal questions. For much of the night, she'd thought about what Jamie had said about how Harrison had been through a lot. She was sure it had to do with his mother, but Nyla didn't ask. Her nosiness was always a cause for contention with her siblings, and she didn't want to show him that side of her. At least not yet. Hopefully, one day she'd get him to open up to her.

"Why'd you sell your car? Are you planning to buy a new one?" Harrison asked.

Well, if he was going to ask questions of her, that was just the opening she needed to ask him a few things.

Instead, she said, "In the future, but not right now. I'm saving to buy Moody Days."

"Really?" Harrison divided his attention between her and the road.

"Yup. Not the building, but the business itself. Gordon, the owner, told me a couple of years ago that he'd sell me the club if I wanted it once he was ready to retire. Back then, it hadn't sounded like that would be anytime soon, but I started saving anyway. I worked a couple of jobs and started stacking my money. I also learned everything I could about the business.

"But then recently, Gordon told me he planned to retire this spring. I saved up a nice chunk of change, but I thought I had more time. So, I sold my car and made a few more sacrifices."

No way would she tell him that one of those sacrifices included not having her own place. She'd been couch surfing for a while now. Even with that, she still didn't have enough money to cover Gordon's asking price for the club, but there was still time. She was close. At least that's what she kept telling herself because no way had she sacrificed all that she had to miss out on her dream.

Wanting to take the conversation off her, she asked, "Are you married?" She knew the answer because there was no way Jamie would encourage her to get to know Harrison better if he was. Still, with her history with men, she had to ask.

"I wouldn't be here with you if I was married, and I sure as hell wouldn't have kissed you." Harrison's words sounded like he was spitting gravel. Clearly, she had hit a nerve.

Nyla turned slightly to better face him and said, "I didn't mean to offend you. It's just that I dated a married man who I hadn't known was married. I have to ask those types of questions, because I don't want to repeat that mistake. Not that I'm saying anything is developing between us. It's just umm... You know what, I'm going to stop talking now." She turned to face the windshield and gritted her teeth to keep from doing more rambling.

"You were involved with a married man...and didn't know it?" Harrison asked, splitting his attention between her and the road. Even though it was dark inside the vehicle, she didn't miss the way his eyebrows pinched together. "Is that what happened?"

Nyla huffed out a sigh. "Yes." That had been before her last relationship.

She didn't embarrass easily, but her cheeks heated, and she felt like an idiot as she told him the story. She and the guy she'd dated before John had lived together for almost a year before she'd known he was married. He and his wife had been legally separated, but still, had Nyla known, there was no way she would've been with him.

Some days she still couldn't believe how long it took her to learn the truth. Hearing herself tell the story out loud made her feel like a dweeb all over again.

"Damn," he mumbled under his breath. "I'm sorry you went through that. The asshole should've been honest with you from the beginning."

She glanced at him. Streetlights filtered through the window as he drove, and splashes of illumination lit his handsome face. There was no judgment in his tone, but she'd wanted to see his expression. The few people who knew—her family—judged her. Maybe Harrison was trying to be nice because they were confined to the truck.

"Well, if it makes you feel any better, I was engaged once, but when I went to prison for first-degree murder, she dumped me."

Nyla's mouth dropped open, and then she burst out laughing. "Okay, that's a good one. If you were trying to make me feel better, it worked."

When he didn't laugh, and he didn't look at her, Nyla's laughter halted immediately. Unease clawed through her veins as she waited...and waited for him to say, just kidding.

When he didn't, she braced herself, then asked, "You're kidding, right?"

Chapter Seven

Harrison gripped the steering wheel tightly enough to break it as he stared straight ahead. First, he screwed up and kissed Nyla before thinking about what he was doing. Now each time he glanced at her, flashes of their heated kiss sent warmth shooting to every cell in his body.

If that weren't enough, after the most amazing kiss he'd experience in like forever, he offered her a ride home. In doing so, he failed to remember he'd be in a confined space with her. That was a problem because she smelled incredible, like lavender and vanilla. He not only wanted to bury his nose into the crook of her neck for a better whiff, but he wanted to explore the rest of her body.

Now this.

He never meant to say anything about his stint in prison. Hell, he never slipped up regarding that time in his life, and he couldn't figure out how he'd done it now. One minute, he was hearing the self-deprecating tone in her voice as she told him about her loser ex. The next? He was telling her he'd been in prison for murder.

Harrison shook his head. He could feel Nyla's heated gaze on him, and it was the oddest sensation. In one sense, it was as if her soft hands were on him, caressing his skin and comforting him in some way. But it also felt as if large hands were squeezing his neck and cutting off his air supply.

His heart was beating hard enough to beat right out of his chest, and the last thing he intended to discuss was that horrible time in his life. Yet, he knew he had to say something. *Anything.* But what could he say after dropping that bomb?

"I shouldn't have admitted to that," he said, his mind scrambling as he maneuvered his SUV through her neighborhood.

"So, it's not true?"

After a slight hesitation, he said, "It is, but Nyla it's not something I can discuss right now. All I can tell you is that I *didn't* kill anyone."

"I know," she said quietly.

He glanced at her. "What do you mean you know? How do you know?"

"Because Jamie thinks very highly of you, and he wouldn't have tried to push us together if he thought you'd be a danger to me. Also, though I don't trust my intuitions as much as I used to, I honestly don't believe you're capable of murder. Remember, I've worked with you for a couple of months. You don't give off killer vibes."

Harrison nodded and released a slow breath as his heart rate slowly settled down. If only his mother and ex-fiancée had given him that same benefit of doubt when he'd been accused.

He wanted more than anything to get to know Nyla better, but it was a bad idea no matter how he looked at it.

Yeah, he needed to stay clear of the beautiful Nyla.

A few minutes later, he pulled into the circular drive of her apartment complex and stopped just past the front entrance.

Part of him wanted to tell her everything. The other part of

Believing in You

him wanted to keep his mouth shut. He had vowed to never mention those days ever again. He almost didn't survive the experience, and as the memories filled his mind, the anxiety was there too.

Nope, this wasn't something he could discuss.

Harrison startled when Nyla laid a hand on his forearm and squeezed.

"I'm sorry if I stirred up bad memories. Are you going to be okay to drive home? Do you want to come in?"

This woman...

This sweet, gorgeous, kind woman. If only he could've met her years ago. Maybe his life would've taken a different route. Then again, maybe it wouldn't have, but deep down, he knew if he allowed Nyla into his life, his world would change for the better.

I'm not ready, the words blared through his mind.

Instead of telling her that, he said, "Thank you for understanding." He squeezed her hand. "I'm fine to drive, and I'm sorry about...everything."

She nodded and gave him a smile as she removed her hand from his arm.

Harrison immediately felt the loss, and he hated the chill that flowed through his veins. He knew this was goodbye, at least on his end. Tonight let him know he wasn't ready to put himself out there again.

"No apology necessary," Nyla said as she unfastened her seatbelt. "Just know if you ever want to talk, I'm a good listener. As a matter of fact, give me your phone."

Instead of overthinking the request, Harrison pulled the device from his pants pocket and unlocked it. Then he handed it to her and watched as she added her telephone number.

"Now you have no excuse if you want to give me a call

outside of work," she said, returning his cell phone. "Take care, Harrison. See you in the morning."

She started to open the door, but he stopped her. "Hold on, let me get that for you."

He climbed out, shivering as the brisk air whipped around him as he hurried around to the passenger side. When he opened the door, he reached for Nyla's gloved hand and helped her out.

"Thanks again for the ride."

"My pleasure," he said, and was caught off guard when she placed a soft kiss on his lips. "Drive safely."

Harrison waited until she was inside before he climbed back into his SUV. On his way home, thoughts of Nyla and how he'd handled everything tonight played on loop inside his head.

If ever he got himself emotionally together, and was ready for a relationship, he'd choose her in a heartbeat.

Too bad he may never be ready.

* * *

Damn him for avoiding her! Nyla never thought of Harrison as a wimp, but this morning she knew better. All night she'd been worried about him, hoping he was okay.

She had even considered calling Jamie to get him to check on Harrison, but she hadn't. Instead, she figured she'd see him this morning at work, except when she arrived at Telecom Solutions, Harrison was a no show. He was working from home.

That rat! He knew I'd have questions.

She should call and curse him out for not being man enough to face her. She wouldn't, but she should.

The only thing stopping her was that he didn't owe her anything. Not an explanation. Nothing. His secrets were his.

Well, she also wouldn't call him because she didn't have his phone number. Yes, she had given him hers, but she hadn't thought to text or call herself while she had his phone in hand.

Then again, that probably wouldn't have been a good idea anyway. He'd seemed to be in a state of shock after dropping his bomb. He might've freaked if he knew she had his phone number.

"I should've done it anyway," she grumbled as the office phone rang.

She answered and then directed the call to the tech support department, all the while still contemplating what to do about Harrison.

It wasn't his fault that she suddenly wanted to know everything about him. She had even considered googling him but shot that idea down. Anything she learned about him, Nyla wanted the information to come from him directly. Or maybe Jamie, but she knew her friend wouldn't betray Harrison's trust by spilling his secrets.

I was engaged once, but when I went to prison for first-degree murder, she dumped me.

Nyla dropped back in her seat and rocked in the chair. Never in a million years did she think she'd hear anything like that come out of anyone's mouth. Let alone Harrison's. A fiancée? Prison? *Good Lord.* She could only imagine what that was all about. It was no wonder he hadn't wanted to discuss it last night. There was a lot to unpack in just that one sentence.

The desk phone rang again, and Nyla answered. "Good morning. Thank you for calling Telecom Solutions. How may I help you?"

There was a slight hesitation before the caller said, "May I speak with Harrison Grant?"

Nyla immediately went on alert. It was the same woman who'd called the day before. Harrison's mother.

"I'm sorry, he isn't in. May I take a message?" Nyla asked instead of sending her to voicemail. She grabbed her notepad and pen, poised to write down the message.

"Do you know when he'll be in?"

"I do not," Nyla said.

The woman huffed out a frustrated breath. "That's okay. I'll try back another time." She disconnected the call before Nyla could respond.

Nyla replaced the headset and growled under her breath. What the hell had his mother done to him to warrant Harrison ignoring her calls? And did she have anything to do with the ex-fiancée... or worse, him going to prison?

"*Ughhh*," Nyla grumbled under her breath.

Harrison Grant, what the hell is your story?

Chapter Eight

Seven days. It had been seven days since Harrison had seen Nyla, and he was having withdrawals. He wasn't sleeping well. His focus at work was shot, and all he wanted to do was call her.

He couldn't.

He couldn't give her mixed signals. She deserved better.

He thought for sure she'd hunt down his phone number and call him. She hadn't. Part of him had been relieved, but the other, twisted part of him, had wanted her to call.

How messed up was that? He had issues. Even he could admit to that.

Not showing up for her last two days of working at Telecom had been a punk move. But after deciding he wasn't looking to get involved with anyone, he hadn't wanted Nyla to stay in touch.

No way would he lead her on if he knew in his heart, he couldn't be all in. Even knowing that, though, his feelings for her hadn't subsided. They had a connection that he honestly didn't want to ignore. If anything, he was more curious than ever about her.

Besides owning Moody Days, what other dreams did she have? How would it be spending weekends roaming the city with her? What would it be like to fix a romantic dinner for her? Would she like that, or would she be like his ex and prefer going to a fancy restaurant so she could be seen?

One question after another had bombarded him, and...

Harrison growled under his breath. "Just stop thinking," he grumbled into the quietness of his office.

As the director of software engineering at Telecom, he didn't have time for lingering thoughts of Nyla. He had two meetings this morning, as well as a major report to complete before the end of the week.

His attention went back to his computer screen, but before he could add to the project status report, a knock sounded on his closed office door, and he welcomed the interruption.

"Come in," he called out, assuming it was their administrative assistant.

Emily opened the door and stepped in with a white shopping bag, and Harrison noted his favorite Italian restaurant's logo on the side of it. The efficient fifty-eight-year-old grandmother of two had been with the company since before Harrison started. Her sparkling gray eyes twinkled as if she knew a secret.

Harrison frowned and stood from his seat. He hadn't ordered lunch, but now that the aromas from the bag filled his nostrils, he realized he was hungry.

"This came for you," she said, holding up the large bag. Then she held out an envelope with the other hand. "It came with a note."

Harrison eyed the bag and the note wearily. His first thought was to tell her to toss both into the trash because it was

Believing in You

probably from Veronica, his ex-fiancée. She'd been calling his cell phone lately, something she did every few months for the last few years. He wasn't sure why since they had nothing to discuss. Like usual, he let her calls go to voicemail before deleting them. However, in all the while they'd been together, he couldn't ever remember her having lunch delivered to him.

Harrison accepted the envelope, and Emily set the bag on the desk.

"I'm heading to lunch. Do you need anything before I leave?"

"No, I'm good. Enjoy your lunch," he said absently as she strolled out of the office while he pulled the note from the envelope.

Harrison, I know you're avoiding me. I'm not sure why. In any event, since you haven't been back to the club for me to thank you properly with drinks, I decided to send you lunch. Thanks for dropping me off at home last week. I hate I didn't get to say goodbye to you before I left Telecom, but I wish you all the best. Nyla.

Aww, hell. Now he really felt like an ass.

As he dug through the bag, he couldn't help thinking this was the nicest thing anyone had ever done for him. The savory aroma of oregano, garlic and basil had his stomach growling in anticipation.

When he removed the lid from the carryout container, Harrison inhaled deeply. Stuffed manicotti, one of his favorite dishes. Not even Jamie knew that. So, Nyla had chosen well.

As he stared down at the food, that also included a small salad and Italian bread, guilt swirled inside of him. He'd done all he could to avoid Nyla and the jazz club. Yet, she'd thought enough of him to send him lunch.

Harrison reclaimed his seat and dug in. After several bites, his eyes drifted closed, and he savored the tender noodles and mouthwatering flavors. The dish was even better than he remembered.

Most days he ended up skipping lunch because of being so engrossed with work. This was a nice treat all the way around, and he needed to thank Nyla.

He was halfway through his meal when his cell phone rang, and he picked it up from his desk. Glancing at the screen, he was surprised to see his sister's name. She was the only one in his family who he still had a relationship with.

"Hey there," he said around a mouthful of food.

"Hi, Harrison."

Harrison's fork stopped midway to his mouth, and the food he'd just consumed sat in his stomach like a three-ton boulder. Anger stirred within him, and he debated on whether to say anything or just hang up. The only thing keeping him from doing the latter was the fact that his mother was calling from his sister's cell phone.

"Where's Piper?" he asked, unable to keep the impatience from his tone.

"She's in the kitchen. She doesn't know I used her phone to—"

Harrison ended the call, effectively cutting off anything else she had to say. He hadn't spoken to his mother in over four years. Not since she turned her back on him when he needed her to believe in him. Though he wanted to forgive and forget, he hadn't.

No longer hungry, he placed the cover back over his food and stuffed everything into the bag. Setting it on the edge of his desk, he struggled to get his mind back on work. The last thing he wanted to think about was why he cut ties to his mother, but hearing her voice brought it all to the forefront of his mind like a ferocious fire destroying everything in its path.

Why would she call him?

He had told her the last time they talked that he never wanted to hear from her again. Surely, she had to know her calling out of the blue would tilt his world on its axis. Knowing her, she didn't care. All she cared about was herself and his brother Geoffrey. It had always been like that, and Harrison had...

"Nope. Not going there." He wasn't letting her ruin his day after receiving such a nice gift from Nyla.

When his cell phone rang again, he didn't bother looking at it. Right now, there was only one person he should reach out to, and that was Nyla.

He picked up his cell phone and called her, only to get her voicemail.

Hi, you've reached Nyla. Unfortunately, I can't take your call at this time...

His heart softened at hearing her sweet voice. At first, he was going to hang up and try again later, but at the last minute, he changed his mind.

"Nyla, this is Harrison. I received the lunch and wanted to let you know how much I appreciate it. Thank you. I can't remember the last time anyone did anything so thoughtful for me. I appreciate your kindness, even though I don't deserve it. Take care."

He disconnected the call thinking he should've said more. Maybe even ask her out to dinner. Thankfully, before he fell down that *would've, should've, could've* rabbit hole, another knock sounded on his door.

"Come in," he called out. When he glanced up, he was surprised to see his boss.

"Sorry to interrupt," Royce Garrison said. Dressed in a dark suit and tie, Harrison assumed he must have a meeting with a client at some point in the day.

"May I come in?"

Harrison stood. "Of course. I would've come to you if I'd known you wanted to talk."

Royce waved him off, then unbuttoned his suit jacket before claiming one of the striped, upholstered chairs in front of the desk.

"I just returned from a meeting and figured I'd stop by before going to my office. Do you have time for us to talk for a minute?"

Harrison reclaimed his seat and leaned back in his chair wondering what was up. They had a great relationship, but he couldn't remember the last time Royce had come to his office. "Definitely. Is everything all right?"

"Everything is great. I just finished meeting with Yancey Jones, and we got the contract."

Harrison grinned. This was a big deal. Jones had been stringing them along for months while he waffled between going with three other companies that all promised to overhaul his company's current, inefficient computer network. Telecom Solutions was the best choice for them and would make the system more dependable, as well as user friendly.

"That's great. Congratulations."

"Thanks. Couldn't have done it without your help, but that's not what I wanted to talk to you about." Royce draped an arm on the back of the other chair next to him. "I have a proposition for you."

It would be hard to say no to whatever his boss asked of him. Royce had been there for him when trouble clouded Harrison's life, and he'd been accused of an unthinkable crime. His boss stood by him and saved his job, his loyalty never wavering.

Harrison leaned forward. "What's up?"

"I want you to run Telecom Solutions here in Chicago," Royce said, a smile wavering on his lips.

Harrison frowned. "I don't understand." They only had one location, unless...

"I'm moving back to Cincinnati to join my family's construction company."

Jenkins & Sons Construction was well-known in Ohio, and the family-owned company was building a reputation of being the best in the Midwest. It had been started by Royce's grandfather, Steven Jenkins, and when he retired, the granddaughters took over and expanded the business. Now, the company was mostly run by all the grandkids.

Royce often mentioned his cousins, and there were a ton of them who were all close. Still, Harrison was surprised Royce was leaving Chicago.

"What about your brothers?" Though Royce owned Telecom Solutions, his two brothers played major roles in the company. Why wouldn't he have one of them oversee operations?

"They're also moving back to Cincinnati. I'm not sure what roles they'll be playing at J & S, but since my mother moved a few months ago, we're all planning to follow her lead."

Royce explained that Jenkins & Sons was adding a tech division that he'd oversee, and he sounded excited about the position. He also talked about how life was short, and family was everything. He wanted to live closer to his extended family and felt this was an opportunity he couldn't pass up.

Harrison was happy for him, but he'd be lying if he said he didn't envy his boss and his relationship with the Jenkins family. That was something Harrison had always wanted, a large, close family who had each other's backs. Something he would never get to experience.

"You know everything about Telecom, and I'd like for you to run it. That'll mean a raise and a bigger office."

"And more responsibilities," Harrison added, and they both chuckled.

"Uh, yeah. That part." Royce grinned. "Over the next few months, we can sit down together and see what this will look like going forward. Of course, you can promote or hire whoever you want to fill your current position and any other positions you think will be needed."

For the next half hour, they talked about the changes that were to come. Harrison welcomed the conversation, and it made him think even more about Nyla and what he wanted for his future.

He could learn a lot from the way Royce was making changes in his life, and it was past time Harrison did the same. And he knew just where to start.

Chapter Nine

Nyla snuggled deeper into her heavy coat as she trudged up the walkway to her parents' three-story bed and breakfast. The Chicago Greystone, with its Italian architectural style was gorgeous inside and out and had seven-bedroom suites, a huge eat-in kitchen, dining room, living room, and a library. If that wasn't enough, there was a two-bedroom, two-bathroom innkeeper's cottage directly behind it where her parents lived.

Jogging up the concrete stairs, Nyla entered the enclosed foyer of the B & B. When she opened the interior door, she was immediately greeted with an aroma of something savory and sweet. Hopefully, it was French toast because she could already envision eating the thick slices of sweet bread that tasted of vanilla, cinnamon, whip cream, and maple syrup.

She was getting hungrier just thinking about the delicious treat. Her youngest sister, Dorian, was a master in the kitchen, even if she hadn't had formal training. No matter what she'd prepared, it was guaranteed to be good.

Setting her bag down, Nyla took off her gloves, hat, and

scarf, surprised there was no one at the front desk. She could see the wide stairs that led to the second and third floors, a long hallway to the side of the guest desk and living room to her right. In there, the brick fireplace had a fire going, but no one appeared to be in the room. Besides voices coming from the kitchen, the building was quiet.

Nyla made quick work of shedding her coat, and as she stored the items in the coat closet, she heard footsteps tapping against the hardwood floors. Then her mother appeared from the back of the house where the kitchen was located.

Virginia Priestly, dressed in a nice sweater and pants set with her hair piled on top of her head, was the ultimate hostess. She always greeted everyone with a smile, and it was impossible not to smile back. Some of the stress that Nyla had been carrying around for the last couple of days began melting away.

"Hi, baby. You look tired," her mother said as she wrapped her into a hug.

"Hey, Mom." Nyla's voice was muffled as she held on tightly.

She closed her eyes and breathed in her mother's comforting scent. She was always baking, either for their B & B guests or for the family, and she often smelled like fresh baked bread or something sweet.

"Thanks for the hug. It was just what I needed," Nyla said as she stepped out of her mother's embrace. "I'm surprised you're not at the cottage resting up before you guys start dinner."

"We had a full house this morning and fell behind schedule. Now that everyone is out and about the city, we're playing catch up. I'm glad you stopped by. Dorian is in the kitchen, and your brother said he was going to stop by during one of his breaks. Are you hungry?"

"Definitely."

They started toward the kitchen, but then the front desk phone rang.

"Go on back. Your sister is baking, and I'm sure there's still some breakfast left."

Nyla stopped at the half bath and washed her hands before going to the kitchen.

"Hey, sis. It smells amazing in here," Nyla said, giving her little sister a quick hug, and then smirked at the apron she was wearing that read, *I know what I'm doing. I watched a YouTube video.*

"Hey yourself. I'm glad you're here, so you can help eat up the rest of this French toast. You might want to grab what you want now. You know once your greedy brother gets here he'll eat everything."

Dorian, who was two years younger, had a slightly lighter skin tone, but she and Nyla were often mistaken for twins. They were the same height and size, but Dorian usually wore her hair in long braids.

She had recently started working for the B & B full time after deciding she needed to part ways from her marketing job. Their parents were thrilled to have one of their children help with the operations of the bed and breakfast. Last Nyla heard, Dorian planned to take over the business once their parents retired, which they'd been talking about more and more lately.

"I'm glad I got here before Zion," Nyla said as she prepared a plate, happy to see there were sausages, breakfast potatoes, and fruit to go along with the French toast. She hadn't eaten since the night before, and even then, it had only been finger food at the club.

Lack of food might be why she'd been dealing with a low-grade headache since she woke up. That and maybe the stress of realizing she was still twenty-three thousand dollars short of Gordon's asking price for the club.

The one thing she didn't want to do was take out a loan to buy the business, but it looked like she might have to take out a small one after all. At least her credit was solid, and she shouldn't have a problem getting it, but she couldn't stop thinking about Cree's words from the other day. If Nyla spent her life savings on the business, what would she live on?

Don't give up, a small voice in the back of her mind said.

There were still a few months for a miracle to happen, and since she still believed in them, she'd hope for the best. Currently, her only other option, other than taking out a loan, was to get some of her family to invest.

She shook her head. Nope, she wasn't going that route, and she was going to stop worrying. Starting now.

"Where's Dad?" Nyla asked as she sat at the table. Her father loved staying busy, and knowing him, he was probably somewhere in the house repairing something.

"He was in here a few minutes ago." Dorian grabbed oven mitts and removed what looked like blueberry muffins from the oven. "He's probably working on his to-do list, which he claims is long enough for three people to tackle. Of course, when Mom suggests he hire help, he insists he doesn't need any."

"That sounds like him."

Nyla squinted against the sunlight pouring through the open blinds and right into her eyes. She stood and closed them, and before she reclaimed her seat, her brother Zion strolled into the kitchen.

At six-feet tall and decked out in his police uniform and a dark blue wool beanie pulled low over his eyes, he looked fierce and intimidating. Nyla hated that he was a cop, risking his life to keep the city safe, but from a young age, Zion had proven he'd been born to protect others. That had a lot to do with why he had joined the Marines right out of high school. After leaving the military, he returned to Chicago and became a cop.

"Hey, Peanut," she said, using the nickname he hated, and before she could scurry away from him, he put her in a headlock. She burst out laughing and tried to wiggle free, which was fruitless.

"What's up, little sis?" he said before eventually releasing her.

She swatted his arm and scowled. "You do know I'm older than you, right?" She was four years older, and at twenty-nine, Zion was the baby of the group.

"I know, but you're also shorter," he said and greeted Dorian the same way.

"If you want what I've cooked, I suggest you unhand me boy," Dorian said between giggles as she playfully punched him in the arm.

Once Zion prepared his plate, and Dorian poured coffee for all of them, they joined Nyla at the table. Small talk flowed between them as they played catch up with each other's lives. Unlike some families, they didn't meet up at a set time every week to eat together, but they were all very close. Nyla knew without a doubt that, if anyone needed the other, they were only a phone call away.

"Nyla, I'm glad you stopped by," their mother said when she strolled into the kitchen. "There's someone I want you to meet."

"*Mom*," Nyla groaned and had to stop herself from whimpering.

She should've gone straight to the club. She didn't realize her mother was still on her matchmaking mission determined to see them all married sooner rather than later.

"Not interested," Nyla said around a mouthful of food.

"All I ask is that you meet him." Her mother leaned on the back of one of the kitchen chairs. "That's it. He's a nice, handsome young man. He's new to the city, smart, funny, creative, and he has a good job. Oh, and did I mention he's a cutie-pie? I think you two would be perfect for each other."

Nyla glanced at Dorian. She had gone back to the large center island where she'd been whipping up another batch of muffins. Nyla didn't miss the way her sister kept her head down while trying not to laugh. That meant she'd probably suggested Nyla for whatever their mother was cooking up.

"Why me? You have three other daughters, two who are older *and* unmarried. Why are you asking me? Oh, and you also have a son who you can matchmake. I'm sure he'd love that," she said pointedly, looking at Zion.

"I'm not in this. So keep my name out of your mouth," he said.

Their mother ignored them and kept talking. She rattled off one reason after another of why she thought Nyla would be perfect for the guy. Nyla had to admit, the man did sound intriguing, but instead of saying that, she said, "I'm not interested, Mom, but thanks. And would you look at the time? I should've been gone."

Dorian snorted but then tried covering the sound with a cough.

Zion didn't bother trying to hide his laughter.

"You all laugh, but I'm tired of being invited to my friends' kid's weddings or hearing how they have another grandchild on the way," their mother grumbled. "I didn't go through a thousand hours of labor to bring the five of you into the world to be treated like this. I should have more grandkids by now!"

Nyla tried not to laugh, but she couldn't hold it in. "*Mom, why are you being so extra today?*"

"*Today?*" Dorian said, still cracking up. "This is a daily occurrence of her bringing up the subject. And she's so busy that when more grandkids do come along, she'll probably be too busy to even babysit."

"I won't! I promise I'll babysit whenever I'm needed. Try me," their mother insisted. "Okay, so Nyla. What day would be good for..."

"I can't. I'm already seeing someone," Nyla bit out, then immediately regretted saying anything. Three sets of eyes were looking at her, and she already knew the questions would start flying thanks to her little white lie.

But was it really a lie?

While she worked at Telecom, she and Harrison had gotten to know each other. Sort of. And though it might've been over a week ago when he kissed her and gave her a ride home, that had to count for something. Right? Not only that, but he had also left her a voice message to thank her for lunch the other day. Surely, that meant they were sorta kinda seeing each other. Even if she still hadn't talked to him because she'd gotten his voicemail when she returned his call.

"What?" she said defensively as her family continued to stare. "Y'all act like I can't get a man."

"We're not saying that, dear," her mother said soothingly, though she didn't look convinced. "But you haven't brought anyone around, and—"

"What's his name?" Zion interrupted, looking at her through narrowed eyes.

"None of your business. No way am I telling you anything just so you can run a background check on him." Nyla stood with her empty plate.

As the words about the background check left her mouth, she remembered what Harrison had said about going to prison for murder. She still didn't know the details, and considering how he'd been avoiding her and the club, she might never know. And she didn't want Zion or anyone else digging into Harrison's background.

"You know what? Fine!" their mother snapped and mock

pouted. "You don't have to make up lies just to get out of going on a blind date. I'll just get used to the fact that I might never have more grandkids."

Nyla rolled her eyes and caught her siblings doing the same as their mother went on and on. They'd heard the speech a million times, could probably recite it word-for-word while also adding the defeated expressions she was making.

Dorian was right. It did seem like their mother was on them even more than usual about settling down and having a family. It probably had a lot to do with Nyla's nephew being seventeen and preparing to go to college in the fall.

Her oldest sister, Essence, had been a teen mom, giving their parents their one and only grandchild. So far, it didn't seem like any of the others were interested in adding to that number.

After hanging out a little while longer at the B & B, Nyla headed to the club. Mentioning Harrison earlier to her family, without actually giving them a name, had her thinking about him. Something she'd been doing a lot of despite trying not to.

She hadn't seen him, but she hoped that maybe he'd stop by Moody Days sometime in the near future.

A girl could hope.

Chapter Ten

This day can't get any worse.

Since leaving her parents' place, Nyla had one issue after another pop up at the club, but this one was the worst.

She propped her elbows on the small oak desk and buried her face in her hands. Her head was pounding despite taking ibuprofen, and at the rate the night was going, it wouldn't be letting up anytime soon.

The only highlight of the day was that it was Friday night, and she had the next two days off. It had been awhile since she'd had the weekend off, and it wasn't a moment too soon. Anything that could've gone wrong today had, and it started when one of her crowns fell off her tooth. Thankfully, she'd found it stuck in a piece of taffy that she'd been enjoying.

No more sticky candy for her. Not only did she have to go in for an emergency appointment at the dentist. She'd also had to dig into her savings to pay for it. Which was the last thing she'd wanted to do.

Now she just found out the trio that she had booked for

tonight's performance cancelled. It wouldn't be a big deal if it weren't for the fact that they were a popular, local group with diehard fans and a huge following. They drew a large crowd wherever they performed, and she was counting on the club being packed tonight.

Sighing heavily, she mentally searched her mind. Where was she going to get another group on such short notice?

"I take it that they canceled."

Dropping her hands, Nyla sat back in her desk chair and glanced across the tiny room. Jamie was leaning against the doorjamb with his arms folded across his chest. He'd been the one to transfer the call to her a few minutes ago.

"Yep, they did. The club is going to be packed with their fans, and I'm going to have to tell them they aren't coming. Worse than that, they were the only performers for tonight."

Some Friday nights, they had a lineup that included as many as three performers, but tonight, she hadn't needed to book anyone else. The leader of the trio had assured her that they could perform three hours with a twenty-minute break in between.

I should have booked an additional group.

"What the heck am I going to do? I know I can't perform all three hours," she said and glanced at the closet door where she had a pants suit hanging.

Since she'd been expecting a large crowd tonight, she'd planned to dress up a little. It looked like she might have to perform, which was something she did on occasion when there was no one else available. Nyla just hoped she didn't get booed off the stage since the customers were expecting a band.

"And even if I could do the whole set, I don't have time to go home and get something more appropriate to wear."

She always carried an extra change of clothes with her.

Usually, casual or workout attire. She hadn't brought anything jazzy enough to be on stage.

Nyla pouted and laid her forehead on the desk. "What am I going to do?" she whined.

"I have an idea. Let me make a call. In the meantime, get dressed. If my plan works, you might still have to perform the first hour, but at least you won't have to do all three."

Nyla lifted her head and frowned. "What's your idea?" she asked skeptically.

Jamie was an advertising agent by day. Maybe one of his clients was in the entertainment industry. But even if she was willing to pay someone, performing for two hours was a lot to ask, especially at the last minute.

"Even if you found someone else, we still have a problem. I can't perform in that stuffy-looking suit," she said.

Jamie waved her off as he headed for the door. "Just wear the jacket and the pants. Leave off the shirt. Then you'll be fine."

Nyla's mouth dropped open as she stared at his retreating back.

The suit was too low-cut to go without the blouse that went with it. Then again, she did have on a red satin bra. If she kept the top button of the suit jacket unfastened, a little of the red would show, and her 36Ds were guaranteed to make the outfit look sexy.

Sighing, Nyla resigned her fate. She was playing tonight.

She groaned in frustration but went back to the computer monitor where she'd been reviewing the liquor inventory. But then she remembered she'd forgotten to ask Jamie about today's shipment. The numbers were off, and he'd been the one to accept the order.

I'll just ask him later.

When she started scrolling down the inventory list, the computer screen suddenly went black, and Nyla froze.

"Okayyyy. What's going on?"

She moved the mouse several times before checking to make sure the computer was still plugged in. When she confirmed it was, she started punching keys on the keypad, silently praying the computer hadn't really died.

Nothing.

It was as if the black screen was taunting her, and it took everything within her power not to push the old desktop computer to the floor.

"Gawd! Can this day get any worse?"

Just then, a loud crash came from the kitchen, and she leaped from her seat and ran out the office.

God, please! Don't let anything else go wrong tonight.

* * *

After playing a few numbers on the piano and singing, Nyla was grateful for the applause. She thanked everyone and told them the next act would be up shortly, then left the stage.

Just as her foot landed on the last step, she stopped in her tracks when she saw Harrison. At least she was pretty sure it was him. The man standing in front of her was a sexier version of him if that were even possible.

On his head was a black fedora, tilted slightly and pulled low over his gorgeous eyes. Eyes that were no longer hidden behind black wire-rimmed glasses.

As her gaze traveled over him, she took in the black leather jacket opened to reveal a dark gray T-shirt. Her eyes went lower and noted how good he looked in black jeans that hugged his muscular thighs. But it was the bottom of his pant legs that gave her pause. They were stuffed into untied... combat boots.

Combat boots?
Harrison owned combat boots?
Good Lord. Where was her buttoned-up, conservative, IT guru who was slow to speak and rarely smiled? Then again, she might like this version of Harrison better. His footwear, the hat, and the leather jacket had him giving off serious bad boy vibes, and she was totally feeling it.

His disguise, for lack of a better word, seemed to wipe away his usual guarded persona. In its place was a tall, confident man who *oozed* sex appeal and was sure to turn heads tonight. He definitely had turned hers, and all her girly parts stirred with need.

Her heart fluttered wildly, and heat charged through her body at the way Harrison was watching her. The sexual tension that usually pulsed between them whenever they breathed the same air was back. She felt it to the soles of her feet, and with the heated lust shining in his eyes, she sensed he felt it too.

Why now, though? Why had he been ignoring her when...

Her gaze suddenly took in the two instrument cases he was holding, and her eyebrows shot up.

"Wait." Nyla rushed to him. "*You're* who Jamie got to perform tonight?" Her shock dripped from each word. "I didn't even know you played an instrument."

A slow smile kicked up the corners of his luscious lips, and her breath stilled in her chest. That small gesture lit up all his handsome features, and her ovaries quivered at the sight.

Harrison set the cases down, reached for her hand, then pulled her close, and Nyla didn't object.

"I'm full of surprises," he said and boldly kissed her.

Her eyes drifted closed, and though part of her knew she should pull away and get some answers, she didn't. Instead, she fisted the front of his jacket and took what he was willingly giving.

The kiss had started sweet but quickly heated up as they got lost in the moment. It helped that there was no one in the dimly lit hallway. Just the two of them with their tongues tangling as if it were the most natural thing in the world to be doing.

Nyla had never experienced this type of lure to anyone, and though she didn't want this to end, it had to. She needed answers.

Reluctantly, she slowly broke off the kiss. They were both panting, and Harrison didn't release her. Instead, he lowered his forehead to hers.

"Hi," he said simply, and Nyla couldn't help but smile. He truly was a man of few words.

She leaned back and met his eyes. "Hi. What are you doing here?"

He eased his arms from around her. "Getting ready to do something I haven't done in a long time." He picked up his instruments. "We'll talk in a couple of hours," he said and then jogged up the three stairs to the stage.

Okaaay. She had questions. Lots of questions.

Though she was exhausted and had planned to hide in the office for a little while to get rid of her nagging headache, she made a beeline for the bar. As she approached, Jamie, the sneaky snake, flashed her a grin.

"*Harrison?*" she said, unable to form any other words.

"Yup, he plays the saxophone, the bass, and he played the drums in college. I guarantee customers will be asking for him to return to the stage after they hear him."

Nyla glanced at the stage. "I had no idea." It looked like he was going to start with his bass guitar. The shiny silver instrument looked extremely expensive as it gleamed under the fluorescent lights.

"Of course you didn't have any idea. He doesn't talk about

himself, and very few people know how musically talented he is. Which is something else you two have in common." He sighed loud enough for her to hear him over the chatter around them. "I know I'm sounding like a broken record, but I like the idea of you and Harrison together. Granted, in most areas, you guys are opposites. He's ridiculously neat, and you're...not. He likes order and typically follows a routine. You don't, mostly."

"Hey!" she shoved him with her elbow even though he was telling the truth. Yet, she didn't need the reminder that there were areas in her life that needed some attention.

"Still, you two are just what each other needs. He's wound too tight, and you can loosen him up. As for what he can do for you? He can ground you. Be that stability you need...like an anchor, but without weighing you down. Get to know him, Nyla. You won't regret it."

"*I've tried!*" she snapped. "Jamie, I can't force someone to open up to me. I like Harrison, and I know the feeling is mutual, but I refuse to throw myself at a man." Even if she felt deep in her soul that he would be worth the effort. "The ball is in his court as they say."

Nyla returned her attention to the stage. Her senses came alive when Harrison introduced himself as Dark Knight Rider, and he started playing the instrumental version of "Under Pressure" by Queen and David Bowie.

He looked so relaxed and comfortable on stage, but Nyla noticed he had pulled his hat down even lower, shielding his eyes. Was he really trying to hide himself? Or was the look, the fedora and him dressed in black, just part of his stage persona?

Whatever it was, it worked. The place was packed, maybe even over capacity, and he definitely had the women's attention. The way he was playing the bass, he was owning the moment. Especially when that song rolled into the next, and he started playing and singing Bill Wither's "Ain't No Sunshine."

Nyla's mouth dropped open. *And he can sing?*

So caught up in his rendition of the song, it was easy to forget they weren't the only ones in the building. Nyla felt every note, every chord, and every word to the depths of her soul while his deep baritone carried the melody with such precision.

"Oh. My. God. He's amazing." If she hadn't already been interested in Harrison, this new revelation would've done it.

Jamie laughed. "I wouldn't have asked him to do this if I didn't know how good he was. He used to play in a few clubs while we were in college. He also wrote music. Once he started his career in IT, he didn't play as often, but he still dabbled around a little. He has an impressive music room in his home. You should get him to show it to you."

Nyla glanced at Jamie. "Seriously?" Hell, she could barely get him to talk. What made Jamie think she'd ever get an invite to his house?

Jamie nodded, that cocky grin still firmly in place. "Yeah, I'm serious. Don't give up on him yet. I have a feeling things between the two of you are just getting started. Be open to the possibility."

Nyla didn't respond as she watched Harrison. Him being on stage was a good start at letting her see a different side to him. She also couldn't forget the way he'd greeted her a few minutes ago. Now that? Had definitely caught her off guard. She might be concerned about his mixed signals, but she absolutely couldn't deny the connection that pulsed between them.

"Why hasn't he participated in open mic nights?" she asked. "He's unbelievable."

Jamie's grin slid from his lips, and he shook his head. Whatever he was thinking probably had something to do with what Harrison had admitted the other night.

"A few years ago, he went through some shit, Nyla. I'm

talking *serious* shit. Even after he made it through, he refused to play anymore. He had even mentioned selling his instruments because he didn't think he'd ever have the desire to play again."

"I guess that changed," Nyla said, glancing at Harrison. What a waste of talent it would've been if he'd given up music.

"Yeah, over the last few months, he's been slowly coming back around. Before that, he refused to play in public. I honestly wasn't sure he'd do us this solid, but once I told him you needed him, he agreed." Jamie shrugged and walked away to fill an order.

Nyla's heart melted. Harrison was doing this for her despite vowing to never play in public again. She didn't know how she'd ever repay him because this was one of the sweetest things anyone had ever done for her. Playing on a stage in front of strangers was no easy feat even if you were talented.

Yet, he was doing it anyway.

For me.

Chapter Eleven

He did it. He performed for two hours, and Harrison felt as if he could take on the world. It didn't hurt that he had received a standing ovation, something he never thought he'd experience again.

But it was the intense adrenaline rush coursing through his veins that had him feeling as if he'd tackled and conquered Mount Kilimanjaro. Like nothing was impossible, and he planned to ride this feeling for as long as possible.

When he exited the stage, he spotted Nyla standing in the shadows against a nearby wall. The lights were dim in the hallway, but he could still make out everything about her, including her usual—wearing rings on every finger. But it was her outfit that had him licking his lips.

He'd been shocked earlier to see her in a suit, specifically the jacket that brought attention to her luscious breasts and her narrow waist. But it was the red satin peeking from behind the jacket that had all the blood in his brain rushing lower. She looked hella good and sexier than he'd ever seen her before.

That's why he hadn't been able to resist kissing her. Well, part of the reason. The other reason had been that he'd missed her. He missed her like crazy.

He had finally come to a decision that he could no longer fight. He wanted Nyla in his life. What that would look like, he wasn't sure yet. All he knew was that he needed to start living in the present. That included getting to know Nyla on a different level. Jamie's phone call hours ago, telling him that Nyla needed him had been just the push he'd needed.

"Hi," Nyla said and shoved away from the wall.

Harrison smiled. The phrase *sight for sore eyes* rushed through his mind because, all the while on stage, he looked forward to being near her again.

"Hey," he said, but as she moved closer, his smile dropped and concern clawed through him. "What's wrong?"

Normally when he saw her, her pretty brown eyes held a spark of mischief or wonder. Not tonight. Though her smile was still in place, it didn't reach her eyes, and the light that usually shone brightly through them was gone.

Needing to touch her, Harrison set his instrument cases down and reached for her hand. He was glad she allowed him to pull her close and when he did, he wrapped his arms around her. Without a word, Nyla snuggled against him, holding on tightly.

"Are you feeling okay?" he asked, loving the way she melted into him, her head resting against his chest.

She fit so perfectly in his arms. It was as if her body was made for him, and he didn't want to let go.

He placed a kiss against the side of her forehead. "Talk to me," he said, feeling like a hypocrite since he'd put off talking to her. "Are you okay?"

After a slight hesitation, she said, "It's been a long, shitty day, and I'm tired."

She took so long to say anything else, he didn't think she would continue, until she lifted her head and looked at him.

"You're very handsome with your glasses on, but without them, you're downright *hot*."

Stunned by her words, Harrison sputtered a laugh. "Umm...thank you?"

She grinned and some of her sparkle was back, but she still looked worn out. "Besides paying you, I don't know how I'll ever be able to thank you for filling in tonight, especially at the last minute. You were spectacular out there."

"First of all, you don't have to pay me. I'm glad I could help. Secondly, it was fun, and that's something I thought I'd never say again about being on stage. Technically, I should be thanking you."

She gave a sad smile and eased out of his hold. "I don't know the details about why you stopped playing but just know that you're welcome on our stage anytime. I mean that, Harrison. Anytime you want to flex your musical talents in front of a crowd, or if you just want to hang around other musicians, you're more than welcome here."

He nodded. As long as he didn't think about the number of people in the audience, or that someone could be posting his act on social media, he might take her up on her offer. He never, ever, wanted to see his face or name splashed on any media outlet. While on stage, he had gotten so lost in his music that hadn't been a concern. The experience tonight felt like old times.

"Thanks," he said. "I'll keep that in mind. In the meantime, do you have to lock up tonight?" He had an idea, and he wanted to present it before he chickened out.

"No. Gordon, the owner, is here and agreed to lock up." She suddenly closed her eyes and rubbed her temples.

"Headache?"

"Yeah, it's been bothering me off and on all day. I'm sure once I get home and relax a little, it'll go away. It's just been one of those days. Anything that could go wrong, did. I'm just… done."

Harrison knew she was tired, but he selfishly wasn't ready for them to part ways. He was ready for them to talk and get to know each other better. Even if it meant telling her about his past. But by the looks of her, tonight might not be the best time for such a heavy subject.

"Are you ready to get out of here?"

"More than ready," she murmured and pushed away from the wall.

"Before I drive you home, how about coming over to my place? I know it's late, but maybe I can fix us something to eat, and we can finally talk."

Seconds ticked by as she studied him, and just when he thought she would say no, she said, "Okay."

The word was spoken so low that, at first, he thought he had misheard her, but then she spoke louder.

"Give me five minutes to grab my stuff."

Chapter Twelve

"Your home is beautiful," Nyla said when they entered Harrison's gorgeous, brightly lit, eat-in kitchen. From where she stood, the open floor plan also gave her a view of the living and dining room.

"Thank you." He stored his keys in a bowl on the counter before he moved through the first floor turning on lights. "Make yourself at home."

It had only taken fifteen minutes to get to his house, and he lived only half a mile from her parents' B & B.

Feeling a little better than she had before leaving the club, Nyla couldn't wait to shed her clothes and make herself a little more comfortable. On the ride there, Harrison had offered to take her home if she was too tired to hang out, but there was no way she'd miss an opportunity to spend time with him. He really surprised her when he told her that, if it got too late, she was more than welcome to spend the night. In his guest room.

He didn't know it yet, but she planned to take him up on his offer. Jamie trusted Harrison, and so did she. Still, she shot off a quick text to her friend, letting him know she was staying the night at Harrison's. Since she still lived with Cree, she also texted her, letting her know she wouldn't be home tonight.

"I'm going to change clothes, then get started on something for us to eat," Harrison said. "Do you need anything before I head upstairs?"

"Actually, I'm going to take you up on your offer of the guest room, if the offer still stands. And if it does, I'd like to change clothes too." She lifted her bag, glad she had gym clothes inside of it. "I think I've had enough of this suit."

Harrison gave her a rare smile and slipped his arm around her waist giving her a good whiff of his magnificent cologne. The woodsy fragrance mixed with a hint of leather was different from what he usually wore. It was downright intoxicating. He brushed his soft lips against her cheek, then nuzzled just below her jaw, and sent a frisson of desire pulsing through her.

Tonight, he possessed a sexual magnetism that highlighted his self-confidence. Nyla was truly seeing a different side of him, and she liked it. A lot.

"If it's any consolation, you look stunning and sexy as hell in this suit."

Warmth spread through her body at the compliment. She hadn't missed the way he'd checked her out before his performance and afterwards. That alone had her thinking about updating her wardrobe. Maybe it was time to ease up on the grunge look. Not totally, but just a little. She'd heard variety was the spice of life.

"Thank you," she said, sure her cheeks would be red with a blush if it weren't for her dark skin.

"Follow me." He carried her bag up the stairs instead of the instruments that he'd brought into the house.

She couldn't wait to see the rest of his home. Nosy? Definitely. Who wouldn't be? Not only was she seriously attracted to the elusive man, but from what she'd seen so far, his home was wonderful.

Harrison pointed to the door on the right—his bedroom. A quick peek inside showed a huge bed in the center of the space and a small sitting area off to the side. The next was the guest room where he set her bag on the bed. It was average size and brightly decorated with an ensuite.

"Since we're up here, let me show you the rest of the second floor before you change clothes."

They passed a guest bathroom, and then they stepped into a slightly smaller room.

"Whoa!" Nyla gasped as she moved farther into the space.

She took in the two televisions, or maybe they were monitors, one on the far wall and one on a gaming-like desk. Clear LED light strips were strung close to the ceiling and went all around the room. Another set of lights were along the baseboards, and both cast a fun glow around the space. On the side walls were glass-enclosed cabinets that held action figures and other gaming equipment.

"This is cool."

"Thanks. Are you a gamer?" Harrison asked, hope filling his tone.

"No, but this space makes me want to be," Nyla said honestly. She had to stop herself from roaming around and touching everything like a little kid.

Harrison chuckled. "Maybe one day I can introduce you to gaming."

She glanced at him and smiled. That told her this wasn't a one-time visit. Whatever this was building between them might have a chance. She couldn't wait to find out.

They moved back into the hallway and went to the last room on the left where the door was closed. Harrison pushed it open, and she had no words.

The music room.

Jamie hadn't exaggerated. The space was a musician's dream. He had truly gone all out in setting up the space. The color scheme of black, gray, white with pops of light blue was gorgeous. A long, overstuffed, gray sofa at one end of the space made her want to lie on it and take a long nap. The rest of the room included a large keyboard, electric drums, and a stand that held a couple of saxophones. Hanging on the far wall were three guitars.

Nyla turned to Harrison. "If I lived in a place like this, I'd never leave home."

He grunted. "I pretty much didn't for the last few years," he said, and invisible shutters covered his eyes. His previous relaxed demeanor was replaced with his usual somber aura. "Why don't you get changed, then meet me downstairs."

While taking a quick shower, Nyla couldn't stop thinking. After touring Harrison's home, it became even clearer that he was so far out of her league. Educated, great job, nice cars, and a gorgeous home, and what did she have? She had money in the bank, but all of it was earmarked for the club. Other than that, she had nothing. What could Harrison possibly see in her?

Jamie had said she and Harrison could be good for each other, but doubt was starting to settle in. They were as different as winter and summer. Surely, once Harrison got to know her better, he'd want to be with someone who was his equal in every area.

But what she couldn't deny was that invisible pull she felt whenever she and Harrison were together. Each time she saw him, she wanted to touch him, kiss him, hug him, and it was obvious he was feeling the same way. His unexpected kisses kept catching her off guard, but was all that enough?

Nyla never considered herself an overthinker. Normally she was a one-day-at-a-time person who rolled with whatever was brought her way. Yet, dealing with Harrison had her thoughts and emotions all over the place.

Once she was showered and changed into yoga pants, a long sleeve T-shirt, and thick socks, Nyla headed downstairs. She was a night owl, but the queen size bed in the guest room was calling her name. She resisted.

"Hey," she said when she reached the kitchen. She sat at the center island on one of the barstools.

He glanced over his shoulder. "That was quick. Do you need medicine for your headache?"

"No. I took something before leaving the club. It's better."

She'd been pushing herself hard the last few weeks, and the long days had caught up to her. She planned to spend the weekend relaxing.

"Hopefully, some food and rest will help," Harrison said as if reading her mind.

His cell phone, sitting face down on the center island, rang, and he lifted it. After a quick glance and a frown at the screen, he silenced the device. Then he shoved it into the front pocket of the well-worn blue jeans he had changed into.

Nyla admired the way his long-sleeve T-shirt molded over his muscular body. The material was thin enough for her to see his sinewy muscles contract with every move he made. She'd seen so many different sides of him, including his styles of dress, since meeting months ago, and so far, she liked what she saw.

As she watched him move around, it was safe to say Harrison felt comfortable in the kitchen. He seemed more relaxed than she'd ever seen him. Clearly, his home was his happy place, but why was she there? Why did he invite her to his home?

So much for not overthinking.

They hadn't talked since the night he'd dropped her off at

home. Yet, today, it was as if no time had passed between them, and that kiss earlier? Goodness. Yeah, they shared an addictive physical attraction that neither of them seemed to be able to resist. The man was downright enticing, but...

"What are we doing, Harrison?" she asked, just as he started cooking grilled cheese sandwiches. He had no idea they were one of her favorite comfort foods. "Why did you invite me over? Days ago, I was under the impression you didn't want anything to do with me."

That stopped him, and he swung around to face her, a spatula in his hands.

"I want everything to do with you," he said with conviction, and her pulse quickened. "You're all I've been able to think about this past week, Nyla. Hell, even longer than that. I'm sorry if I'm throwing out mixed signals, but I needed to get my head straight before I could come to you correctly."

He turned back to the stove to flip the grilled cheese and turned off the tomato bisque he had going. Then he returned his attention to her.

"You came into my life when I was just resurfacing, for lack of a better word. I don't think you understand how strong of an effect you have on me. You make me want things that I haven't wanted in a long time. Things I never thought I could have, and I wasn't ready."

Nyla wasn't normally speechless, but this... There was a bit of anxiousness behind his statements. As silence filled the space and as she dissected his words, he turned back to the sandwiches.

He hadn't been ready for her. If she took time to think about it, she could say the same about him. For the last couple of years, her focus had been on buying Moody Days. She'd worked day and night, planning, saving, and a whole lot of praying that she could pull this off. She honestly didn't have time for a relationship. So yeah, she understood where he was coming from. Still...

Approaching him, she placed her hand on his lower back, and he glanced down at her. "You said you hadn't been ready for me. What changed?"

He plated their sandwiches, and his intense eyes bore into hers. He really was a sexy man, and she was still trying to get used to seeing him without his glasses.

His large hand cupped her cheek as he brushed the pad of his thumb over her skin, and Nyla damn near purred. Her flesh prickled at the tenderness of his touch. For a big, grumpy guy, he had a calm, soothing presence about him, and in this moment, she felt cherished.

Harrison lowered his head and kissed her sweetly. "It's time for me to start living again, and when I picture how that'll look, I see you as part of that vision."

Stunned, Nyla didn't know how to respond. He spoke with such conviction that she believed every word, but they didn't know each other. Not really. All they had going for them was a serious attraction that made her want to be reckless. Something she couldn't afford to be.

However, when had she ever let that stop her?

Chapter Thirteen

Good food.
Good company.
One of the best nights he'd had in a long time, and Harrison wanted more. Mainly he wanted more of Nyla and not just sexually. She was a breath of fresh air and sunshine on a cloudy day combined. He loved her energy, her vibe, and inviting her over had been one of the best decisions he'd made in a long time.

Harrison also loved how she hadn't given him a hard time about not being in the office during her last days at Telecom. He had explained that staying home to work was in the best interest of everyone. He hadn't been in the right headspace after memories of his past came crashing back to the forefront of his mind. That, along with his strong feelings for Nyla, he'd needed time to process it all. Nyla said she understood, and she reiterated that, if he ever wanted to talk, she was there for him.

Part of Harrison's reason for inviting her over was to do just that, talk, and to formally apologize. Nyla suggested they focus on relaxing and enjoying each other's company, and if he wanted to discuss his past, fine. If not, she wasn't going to pressure him.

He glanced at the remains of their meal and smiled. They'd eaten dinner in the living room, picnic style in front of the fireplace with the lights dimmed. They were sitting on the floor where they'd put the sofa cushions, and they used the cocktail table to hold their food and drinks.

Such a simple idea was making for a perfect way to wind down. The only thing that had given Harrison pause was when Nyla suggested they play twenty questions. Something he'd never done, but according to her, it was a way to get to know each other better.

Wasn't that why he'd asked her over? So he could finally share some of his background with her? So they could get to know each other better?

"City living or suburban living?" she asked as she sipped from her wine glass.

"City," he said, though he had grown up in the suburbs. In college and while playing at various nightclubs, he had fallen in love with the city of Chicago's energy. "You?"

"Definitely the city." She gave him a smile that pierced his heart.

Having her sitting next to him like this didn't seem real. He had envisioned what their first date would be like. Dinner at an expensive restaurant, maybe some dancing or a night at the theater, but this was much better. Relaxing. Fun. Romantic.

Harrison marveled at how different she was from other women he'd dated, not that they were dating, but he couldn't help comparing. Nyla was easy to be with, and she outshined them all. Even the woman he'd planned to marry and spend the rest of his life with.

"Chicago style pizza or New York style?" he asked.

"Neither. I prefer Detroit style pizza. Not too flat, not too thick, but just right with the perfect amount of caramelized cheese around the edges." She moaned as if tasting what she had just described, and Harrison felt the erotic sound to the depths of his soul.

Damn. If all it took was a moan from her to make his body stir, then he was further gone than he originally thought.

Okay, maybe playing twenty questions wasn't so bad. In the last thirty minutes, he had learned she was a middle child out of five. Her parents used to work in corporate America, but they left their jobs to open a bed and breakfast. He was familiar with the B & B because the building it was housed in was one of the most beautiful structures in his neighborhood. And now he knew he needed to get her some Detroit style pizza to get her to moan like that again.

"What about you?" she asked.

"Without a doubt, Chicago style. No way I can call myself a Chicagoan and not love all things Chicago, especially the pizza."

They both laughed, and he grabbed his water bottle.

Nyla waved him off. "Yeah, I guess you have a point. Okay, what's your favorite sexual position, missionary or doggie style?"

Harrison sputtered, coughed, and pounded on his chest. He'd just taken a swig of water that went down wrong.

"What?" he croaked, still coughing.

Nyla, grinning, rubbed his back. "Didn't mean to get you all choked up there, Mr. Grant. You okay?"

Harrison dabbed at the corners of his eyes and wiped his mouth with the sleeve of his T-shirt. "Yeah," he said, clearing his throat as he stared at her, not missing the naughtiness swimming in her eyes. "You caught me off guard, but to answer your question. My favorite sexual position is any way I'm buried deep inside of you."

Nyla's eyes grew huge, and her mouth hung open.

"Umm...okay," she said, and lowered her long lashes demurely. Harrison didn't miss the sly smile playing on her tempting lips.

He was sure she hadn't expected that response, but he meant it. When they finally made love, he had no doubt they were going to be electrifying together. This thing between them, this remarkable, mind-blowing, magnetic pull between them was like nothing he'd ever felt. It was exciting while also being scary as hell.

Nyla still didn't respond to his comment. Instead, she drained her wine glass. If she'd been trying to turn him on with her words, her questions, and even her innocent—not so innocent—expressions, it was working.

When he invited her over to his place, it had only been under the purest of intentions, but the more time they hung out, the more those intentions were shifting.

"Kissing in the rain or kissing in a movie theater?" she asked, as if she hadn't just sent his mind on a free-fall, wondering what it would be like to make love to her.

"Hold up. You know it's my turn to ask a question," he said, turning more to face her. "What's your favorite sexual position?"

She nibbled on her lower lip, again looking like she was struggling not to smile. "I'm not sure, yet. Hopefully I'll find out soon."

Harrison's dick twitched. If that wasn't an invitation, he didn't know what was. It was taking all his restraint not to ravish her body, but he couldn't. Not yet. Not until he shared his truth. No matter how emotionally painful it might be, she deserved to know who she was getting involved with.

As if sensing the route his thoughts had taken, Nyla squeezed his thigh. The heat from her touch, even through his jeans, sent an electric current shooting over his skin. It had been a long time since he'd wanted a woman as bad as he wanted this beauty sitting next to him.

Soon. Even if it didn't happen tonight, they'd be intimate soon. Of that he had no doubt.

"Now answer my question. Kissing in the rain or kissing in a movie theater?"

"In a movie theater," he said, clearing his throat that had suddenly gone dry. "I wouldn't want to get my hair wet," he cracked, and ran his hand over his low haircut. She burst out laughing, and he loved the throaty sound of it. "What about you?"

"In the rain, *of course.*" She grinned and shrugged. "I'm a romantic, and I don't care if my hair gets wet."

"Seriously? You don't care if your hair gets wet?"

"Nope."

"And you would risk getting soaked and catching pneumonia?"

"Yup. I'm a risk taker. What can I say? And I'm all for a good, *wet* kiss."

"So am I," Harrison said and slid his hand behind her neck, then covered her mouth with his.

He was game for any type of kiss, wet or otherwise, just as long as the lips touching his belonged to Nyla. Harrison had been wanting to taste her again since arriving at his place, and he was glad she was a willing participant. Her natural sweetness combined with the earthiness of the red wine on her tongue were like an aphrodisiac making him dizzy with desire.

The slow, drugging kiss was as challenging as it was rewarding because Harrison wanted her naked. He wanted to feel, kiss, and touch every part of her luscious body, but the voice in the back of his head screamed—not yet! Not before she knew more about him. He wanted her to have all the information before she decided whether to take a chance on him.

Yet, he couldn't pull away. She tasted too good. Instead, he lifted her onto his lap, and Nyla's arms immediately went around his neck. Their kiss had started out slow but with each lap of their tongues, soul-reaching pleasure stirred within him.

Harrison eased her onto the floor and covered her with his body without breaking their connection. *Gawd, this woman.* She kissed him with a hunger that rivaled his, and their moans mingled, filling the quietness in the room.

As he loved on her mouth, Harrison slid his hand under her shirt and found her skin was as soft as he imagined it would be. Yeah, this was what he wanted. His hand moved up to cup her breast, and Nyla ground against him.

Damn she felt incredible, and his senses went into overdrive, while that nagging voice inside his head kept screaming at him. Harrison ignored it. He moved his lips to her jaw, then beneath her ear, and on down to her scented neck.

"I want you," he murmured against her smooth skin as he tweaked her pert nipple through the satiny fabric. Nyla cried out, and that only turned Harrison on more.

Frantically, he lifted her shirt higher and then her bra. It was as if her perky nipples were begging for attention, and he didn't want to disappoint. His mouth covered one while his fingers tweaked the other.

"*Oh, God.* Harrison," Nyla whimpered and squirmed.

Her hands gripped the back of his head, holding him in place, while her lower body bucked against him. He licked, sucked, teased, and gently bit down on her nipple before moving to the other one. While his tongue swirled around the dark bud, he cupped her other breast, squeezing.

"Oh, my goodness," Nyla murmured, her head brushing back and forth against the rug. "I—I'm not sure I can take much more." Her words were breathy as she continued wiggling beneath him.

Not yet. You can't do this yet! That voice in Harrison's mind hounded him. He tried shushing it, but...

"I want you so damn much," he said on a groan, willing himself to slow down. No. Not. Slow down, he needed to stop.

He cursed under his breath and abruptly rolled off Nyla, bumping into the coffee table in the process.

"I can't," he panted. "We can't do this, not before we talk," he said, his chest heaving as he stared up at the ceiling.

Breathing hard, Nyla scrambled to a sitting position and adjusted her bra and shirt, and Harrison groaned. He'd probably call himself all kinds of a fool later, but right now, his only concern was doing right by Nyla. She had a right to know who and what type of person she was getting involved with.

"I'm sorry, baby," he said, the endearment falling from his lips naturally. "I shouldn't have started—"

"Technically, I'm the one to blame. My round of questioning was suggestive, and I'm sorry about that. I'm not a tease."

Harrison bolted up. "Of course you're not," he said, rubbing his hand down her arm. "I've been wanting to kiss you all night. We only did what came naturally. Unfortunately, Nyla, I don't feel comfortable moving forward until I tell you about my time in prison."

Harrison was smart enough to know that to really move on from his past, he needed to come to terms with it. That meant dealing with his mother and Veronica instead of shutting them out whenever they called. He also needed to share his story with Nyla. She was coming to mean something to him, and they would never have a future together if he couldn't close that chapter in his life. Especially the painful parts.

Closing his eyes, Harrison pinched the bridge of his nose.

He was going to need something stronger than water to get through this conversation. Yet, he also needed to be sober instead of consuming liquid courage.

He startled when Nyla squeezed his hand. "Hey, if you're not ready to talk about it, it's okay. I'll be around whenever you are ready."

Bringing the back of her hand to his lips, he kissed it. "Thank you, but it's time. First, let me clear these dishes and make some coffee. Unless you'd prefer something stronger."

"Water for me, and I can help clean up."

She started to stand, but Harrison encouraged her to relax while he took care of the dishes. It wouldn't take but a couple of minutes to load the dishwasher. He was glad she didn't argue because he needed a few minutes alone.

Harrison made quick work of gathering up their dishes while Nyla pulled the room back together. After taking her a bottle of water, he returned to the kitchen and got to work tidying up. He debated on where to start with the conversation.

How much should he share? It was late. Surely, she wouldn't be up for hearing the whole sordid details of the snowball of events that shook his world to almost disrepair. Then again, if he wanted a future with Nyla, she deserved to know everything.

Sighing, he dried his hands and didn't bother with the coffee. It was now or never. He went back to the living room, then pulled up short. Chuckling, Harrison shook his head.

She's asleep.

Nyla had returned the cushions to the sofa and was fast asleep. What had he been thinking? Of course she was exhausted after her long night at the club. Instead of encouraging her to go to bed, he hadn't wanted the night to end—for any reason.

Starting down at her, Harrison sat on the edge and gently

ran the back of his fingers down her soft cheek. She didn't stir, and he didn't have the heart to wake her. Instead, he stood and swept her into his arms.

"Harrison," she whimpered, and warmth spread through him when she snuggled into him.

This feels right, he thought as he climbed the stairs. Tomorrow. They'd talk tomorrow.

Chapter Fourteen

Tired but not sleepy, Harrison entered his music room with his mind whirling. This was one of the best nights he'd had in a long time, even if it included him contemplating next steps in his life.

He knew a lot of that had to do with Nyla's presence. She made him hope for a better future. She also made him want to deal with and close the door to his past. The first one, he was looking forward to. The latter, not so much. It was going to take some emotional work that wouldn't be easy.

Instead of picking up his bass guitar or sitting at his keyboard, Harrison dropped down onto the sofa and stretched out. The room might be soundproof, but it was too late to fiddle around on any of the instruments. Still, the room always gave him solace. How many days had he sat in here to think about everything and nothing?

"Too many days to count," he murmured as his eyes drifted closed.

He had just gotten comfortable when his phone vibrated in his pocket. Since he knew it wasn't Nyla calling, he started to ignore the call, but he didn't. He dug the device out of his pocket, not surprised to see Veronica's name on the screen. This was her second time calling tonight. She called once or twice a year, but this was the third or fourth call in a matter of weeks.

He sat up and placed his feet on the floor before answering the call. Might as well try to close this chapter in his life once and for all.

"Hello," he answered and was greeted by silence. "Hello?"

"Harrison, I'm—I'm shocked you answered," Veronica said, her voice seductive and breathy. "How are you?"

"I'm fine. Why are you calling, Veronica?"

"To talk. To apologize. To beg you to forgive me for...well, everything."

There was a lot to forgive, but his biggest problem was forgetting. It was hard to forget she'd broken off their engagement when he'd needed her by his side. Which made it hard to forget she hadn't defended him. At least not the way he needed. It was also hard to forget she'd betrayed him by thinking he was capable of killing an innocent woman.

But that was the past, and he was trying like hell to leave everything related to it and her there. That was one of the main reasons he'd shown up for Nyla tonight. He wanted to move forward with his life, and he felt deep in his heart that spending time with her was the first step. He'd wanted her to know he was interested in her. Filling in for her performer who had canceled had been his way of showing her that she could depend on him.

"I'm so sorry," Veronica said, sounding like she meant it. "I know it's too many years too late, but I really am sorry. Deep in my heart, I knew you had nothing to do with that woman's murder, but my family..."

Yeah, she came from old money, and Harrison could almost

imagine her parents telling her that she needed to distance herself from him. Most times, she had a mind of her own, but her family was about appearances. Having a fiancé on trial for murder, whether he committed it or not, wasn't a good look for them.

"I was a fool and let outside sources govern my decisions. Harrison, I'll never be able to apologize enough for not being there for you. Can you ever forgive me?"

"Why now?" Harrison asked.

Sure, she had called him once or twice over the years, but her apologies felt thin, like she had an ulterior motive for saying she was sorry. Tonight, though, it felt more sincere, and he wanted to know what changed.

"What do you mean, why now? I've tried telling you I'm sorry. Ever since you were released from prison, I'd leave voicemails saying as much. Only once did you answer the phone. Unfortunately, as soon as you heard my voice, you hung up. I'm actually surprised you haven't blocked my number."

Yeah, he wasn't sure why he hadn't. Maybe because she hadn't called much until lately.

"Why now?" he asked again.

"Because..." She released a frustrated breath. "Because you've been on my mind lately, and I feel guilty. I always think about you this time of year. If things had worked out between us, last week we would've been celebrating our fourth wedding anniversary."

Harrison sat speechless. He hadn't thought about their wedding date since before he was arrested. It suddenly seemed like a lifetime ago, and he would've been fine not remembering. She had started planning their big day a year in advance. According to her, it was supposed to be the wedding of the century.

He was a simple guy and would've been fine with getting

married in front of a few friends and family. Not Veronica, though. She'd wanted the wedding to be the talk of the town.

Harrison shook his head. He should be thanking her for breaking up with him.

"I still feel awful about the way I handled everything. I know saying I'm sorry will never be enough, but I'm—"

"I accept your apology. It doesn't change anything between us, though," he said, needing to make that clear. There was so much he'd been holding in, and it was time he said what he needed to say to her. "I now know the type of person you are. The type of woman I almost made the mistake of marrying. Thank you for breaking our engagement. It's clear we were wrong for each other."

"Harrison, don't say that. We were great together, and we were once good friends. I was hoping we could at least go back to that. No, I might not have responded appropriately to your... your situation, and I know I didn't do right by you. However, I did what I could. Though I didn't attend every minute of your trial, don't forget I'm the one who hired my family's lawyer to defend you."

Harrison released a humorless laugh. "And we saw how that turned out. I'm not even sure if the guy asked me if I'd done what I was accused of doing. Back then, I was so mentally and emotionally distraught, I hadn't even thought about that.

"It would've been nice to have my fiancée there fighting for me. Someone who claimed to love me and had planned to spend the rest of her life with me. Someone who could've been my mouthpiece when I wasn't able to think straight, let alone express what I needed done. Someone to demand my lawyer look around every corner and under every rock to find the truth.

"It wasn't until after I was convicted did I have the bandwidth to replay all that through my mind. It wasn't until my boss found me a new lawyer, one who dug deep for answers—for the truth—that I realized what a sorry excuse of a lawyer I originally had. I also realized how you failed me. How you didn't love me enough to stand by me."

Silence as thick as a San Francisco fog filled the phone line. Harrison had said more than he needed to and had probably caught Veronica off guard. But he had to share the feelings that he hadn't verbalized to anyone except to his sister and to Royce.

It's all a part of the healing process, his therapist had said so often when he'd have a small breakthrough. Or when he'd question her weekly assignments.

He had met with his therapist for a year after his release from prison. She'd been good at her job, helping him pick up the pieces of his life and rejoin society. Yet, there were some aspects where he hadn't been ready to put in the work. Work that would've helped him come to terms with the pain brought on by those who'd wronged him.

Apparently, he was finally ready to forgive and move on. At least, he hoped that was what was happening.

"I—I don't know what to say," Veronica said after a long hesitation. "I feel awful, and I hope one day you can find it in your heart to forgive me."

"I told you, I have."

"It doesn't sound like it!" Harrison could almost picture the pout that she had perfected. The one where she stuck her bottom lip out slightly and batted her long, fake eyelashes.

Those days of caring what she thought or what she was trying to get were over. *Done.* He was finally moving on, and a weight had been lifted off him. He felt lighter.

When Veronica started saying something else, Harrison cut her off. "Thanks for calling, Veronica. I'm glad we had a chance to talk, but please delete my number from your contacts. We've said all we need to say to each other. Have a good night."

After disconnecting, Harrison released a contented sigh and headed to his bedroom. His therapist's words played on loop through his mind.

It's all part of the healing process.

Now, there were a few other steps he needed to take to rid himself of the burden he'd been carrying for far too long. In the meantime, he'd continue getting to know the beautiful Nyla. He had a feeling being with her was going to be exciting as well as adventurous.

Chapter Fifteen

Good afternoon, Sleepy Head. I hope you slept well. I had to make a quick run to the office, but I'll be back soon. In the meantime, there's breakfast in the kitchen. Make yourself at home and don't leave! Also, in case you need something else to wear, here are some sweats. Remember, don't leave! H.

Nyla laughed and looked down at the red rose that Harrison had left next to the note on top of the clothes. It was after twelve and apparently, she had slept as soundly as usual since she hadn't heard Harrison enter the room.

Don't leave, his words made her smile.

Leaning back against the headboard, she brought the rose to her nose, loving the wonderful fragrance. She was glad Harrison wasn't ready to get rid of her. Spending time with him last night had been just what she'd needed after a long week. It was fun getting to know him. His sense of humor had been on full display, and he'd been a good sport about playing twenty questions.

Then there was that heated kiss they'd shared. The one

that led to heavy petting. Even thinking about it had Nyla squeezing her thighs together to tamp down memories of the delicious ache he'd sparked between her legs.

The man could turn her on with just a look, but having his mouth, his tongue, and his large hands on her body had her wanting a repeat. If he hadn't stopped last night, they would've ended up naked because Nyla had no intention of stopping.

She wanted him. All of him. When he was on top of her, she had felt every inch of his strong, solid body. But it was his thick erection pressed against her lower stomach that almost had her coming without him being inside of her. Even now, it was as if she could still feel his mouth on her. The way his lips had caressed her skin, and the way his tongue had teased each nipple made her...

"Ahh, hell. I need to stop this," Nyla murmured.

Thinking about Harrison, his dick, and that tongue of his wasn't helping. No, she needed to get up, get dressed, and see what was in store for the day. Besides, she needed to mentally brace herself for the talk he'd wanted to have last night.

It had been easy to see that he hadn't been ready to bare his soul to her. Which was why she'd initiated the twenty questions game. She figured she'd give him an out because, whenever he did decide to open up to her, Nyla wanted him comfortable. Well, as comfortable as talking about prison and murder could be.

She stared down at the rose again, and her heart squeezed. What if whatever he told her brought up so many bad memories that he'd retreat from her again? She wanted to see where their attraction could take them, but she knew her heart couldn't take another rejection. Doubts about not being good enough for him were already trying to sneak in, but if his past made him take a step back from her...

"Don't go there," she mumbled. *Just stay in the right here and the right now*, she reminded herself.

She was crazy about the man and didn't want whatever this was building between them to be over before it got started. At least it was safe to say Harrison trusted her. He left her in his home alone, and she was sure that wasn't a norm for him. No, he didn't trust easily, so she'd look at it as progress.

Nyla set the rose on the bed and headed to the attached bathroom. Maybe a shower could help clear her mind. Overthinking was new for her, and she was pretty sure she hated it. She needed to channel her free spirit, go with the flow persona if she was going to enjoy her time with Harrison.

A short while later, Nyla finished rolling up the pant legs and sleeves of the sweats that Harrison had given her to wear and went downstairs in search of a vase. When she finally made it to the kitchen, she couldn't help but laugh. In the middle of the center island was a crystal vase that held at least two dozen roses. Or maybe twenty-three of them since she held one in her hand.

Grinning like an idiot, she hurried to the island and buried her face in the beautiful bouquet. The scent was amazing. Seeing a small card with her name on it tucked between the stems, she plucked it out and read: *Just because...*

Gawd! This man was too good to be true. She loved flowers, especially roses. Sadly, it had been years since she'd received any, and Harrison's thoughtfulness hit her right in the feels. If he was trying to make an impression, it was working. Last night he had her feeling desired, and today she felt treasured.

I'm going to have to do something special for him, she thought as she poured a cup of coffee. There were pastries on the counter and a scribbled note that said fruit and juices are in the refrigerator. There was also a covered dish, and whatever it was smelled delicious. She couldn't wait to dive in, but first, she'd start with coffee.

After adding sugar and Irish cream creamer to the aromatic dark brew, Nyla took a tentative sip and moaned with pleasure. "Excellent."

As she leaned a hip against the counter, she glanced around the open space. The house was quiet, except...

With her mug in hand, she strolled to the window, surprised at all the snow. It had started coming down on their way to Harrison's house, but she hadn't expected to see what looked to be seven or eight inches. What surprised her more was Harrison outside shoveling. He was in the process of clearing the walkway that led to the detached garage.

Nyla smiled as an idea bloomed inside of her. Another few sips of her coffee, and she set the mug down and went in search of her coat and boots. Minutes later, she stepped outside. It wasn't as cold as it had been in the past week, but it was cold enough to have her shivering despite the layers of clothes.

Harrison kept shoveling, then suddenly stopped and turned as if sensing her. A slow smile spread across his mouth, and he let the shovel fall into a pile of snow.

"Hey. What are you doing out here?" he asked and wrapped her in a bear hug. His cold lips met hers and she melted against him.

"I love being greeted like this," she said when the kiss ended.

"Good to know." He gave her another quick kiss. "It's too cold for you to be out here. Head back in the house, and I'll be in shortly."

"Actually, it's not that bad," she lied, wanting to hang out there with him. "If you have another shovel, I can even help."

"That's not necessary, but I welcome the company. I'll make this quick."

He went back to shoveling, and Nyla stuffed her gloved hands in her pockets as she shuffled her feet back and forth to keep warm. More snow had fallen than she originally thought, and it was heavy enough to make a snowman. Actually, it was perfect for a snowball fight, something she hadn't done in a long time.

A grin spread across her mouth, and she quickly made a few snowballs while Harrison's back was turned. His focus was solely on clearing the walkway, and she used that to her advantage.

Six snowballs should be a good start.

Nyla held them all in the crook of her arm, and let one fly, and then another, and yet another. The first two hit him in the back, and the last one splattered on the back of his head. Good thing he was wearing a thick wool cap.

She started grinning when Harrison stopped shoveling and glanced over his shoulder. She threw another snowball at him, and it hit him smack-dab in the middle of his forehead.

Bursting out laughing, she almost dropped her last two snowballs. His incredulous expression only made her laugh harder.

"Seriously?" he finally said, unsmiling and still looking as if he couldn't believe she'd hit him with snowballs.

Unable to help herself, she threw the last two at him. One hit him in the chest, and the other went wide and missed him. Instead of laughing with her, Harrison dropped the shovel and charged toward her.

"Oh no!" Nyla turned to run but had barely taken two steps before she was tackled to the ground. "Ahhh!" she screamed, then turned over onto her back only to be met with a face full of snow.

It was ridiculously cold, but she couldn't stop laughing. Not one of those little giggles, but a full-bodied laugh that had her stomach muscles hurting.

"Harrison, this is not how you have a snowball fight!" Sputtering, laughing, and wiggling against him, she almost got away, but he straddled her.

"Oh, is that what we were supposed to be doing? It was an unfair fight since you just attacked me with snowballs without warning."

"That's how snowball fights work. You attack, then run, but I—I'm sorry."

"I don't believe you. Otherwise, you wouldn't be falling out laughing," he said, a rare smile on his face.

He grasped both of her arms above her head, then held her wrists in place with one large hand. "So, you want a snowball fight, huh?"

He didn't give her a chance to respond. Instead, he smashed more snow into her face causing her to scream and sputter some more.

"Wh—what are you doing?" she stammered while still laughing. Moving her head left and right, she tried to keep Harrison from smothering her with more snow. "You—you, this is not how a snowball fight works."

"Well, this is how I play," he murmured, shoving more snow into her face and a little inside her jacket.

"Oh, my God!" she shrieked, still trying to get free of him while struggling to breathe because she couldn't stop laughing. "Okay. Okay. For real, I'm sorry," she said unconvincingly.

Nyla couldn't remember the last time she'd laughed this hard. Tears leaked from her eyes, probably freezing on her face while her cheeks hurt from all the laughing.

"Okay. Okay. I—I give up," she managed to say.

"Now that's what I like to hear," Harrison said, using the end of the scarf around her neck to wipe her face.

When he smiled down at her, Nyla's heart pounded double-time. The man was so handsome, it was almost hard to look at him. Add that to his thoughtful and kind nature, and she was officially hooked. She more than wanted him. More than wanted to spend time with him, and that excited her while also scaring her a little. What if he realized she wasn't enough for him? Would he be like John? Date her for a while, dump her, and then end up with someone else weeks later?

"You're beautiful," Harrison said just above a whisper, and her thoughts flew away.

He stared at her for a minute before crushing his lips to hers and thrusting his tongue into her mouth. It was as if time stood still and the cold that had been seeping into her body was replaced with a roaring fire. The intensity behind the searing kiss was different from all their other kisses. This one...this one felt as if he was claiming her. As if he was saying, *you're mine. All mine.* Or maybe she was projecting.

But damn the man could kiss.

When he released her hands, needing both of his to hold her, Nyla wrapped her arms around his neck and deepened the connection. The weight of his body on top of hers felt so good, and with the heat pouring from his body to hers, she was sure she could stay like that forever.

Between last night and today, something had definitely shifted between them, and Nyla wanted him even more than she'd wanted him last night. If his potent kiss was any indication, he wanted her too.

Kids' laughter and screaming in the distance met her ears and, apparently, Harrison's too. He slowly ended the kiss and lifted his head. He gazed into her eyes, and without his glasses, she could make out every emotion—joy, excitement, and even vulnerability. More than anything, though, she saw desire.

"I want you more than I've ever wanted anything in my life," he said, and Nyla could feel the deep rumble of his voice to the depths of her soul.

"Then take me," she whispered.

Chapter Sixteen

"Too many damn clothes," Harrison mumbled and was surprised when Nyla bit out a laugh.

He hadn't meant to say that out loud, but it was true. They were in his mudroom, rushing to get out of their outerwear. He finished first, and the moment Nyla took off her boots, Harrison scooped her up into his arms. That made her giggle like a schoolgirl.

"You're incredibly strong," she said, nibbling on his neck and sending heat rushing through his body like a hot soldering iron touching metal.

He was barely staying in control as it was, and the feel of her mouth on his skin had him stumbling on the stairs.

"If you keep that up, we might not make it to the bedroom," he said, but a few seconds later, he made it to the top of the landing.

He wasted no time getting her into the bedroom and setting her on the bed. Her butt had barely touched the mattress before he was on her, kissing her like a starving man needing food.

It had been a long time since he'd been with a woman, and his brain told him to slow it down. Yet the rest of his body screamed, *Hurry the hell up!* But after a few more minutes of feasting on Nyla's mouth, he decided to listen to his brain. No way would he rush their first time together. He intended to cherish *every* moment of getting to know *every* inch of her luscious body.

When Harrison eased his mouth from hers, Nyla whimpered and looked at him as if he had lost his mind. "If you even think about..." Her words trailed off when he leaped up and removed his sweater and T-shirt, tossing them to the floor. Next went his jeans and socks, leaving him in only a pair of black boxer briefs.

"You were saying?"

"I—I..." she stuttered, and her gaze did a slow crawl down his body and then lingered on his shaft that pushed painfully against his briefs. "*Wow,*" she whispered. "Umm, I was saying that I have on way too many clothes."

Harrison grew even harder as she continued her perusal of him while she began stripping out of the sweats that he had given her. They practically swallowed her whole, but when he saw what was hidden under the clothing, his breath stalled in his throat.

Perfection. The woman's curvy body was absolute perfection, and it was clear that she was comfortable in her skin. She wasted no time tossing the satiny white bra and matching panties to the floor.

Mercy.

Flawless full breasts, that were more than a handful, snagged his attention and had him licking his lips. Then his gaze went lower to her narrow waist that flared into hips that he couldn't wait to hold on to.

And then there was the little patch of...

Nyla cleared her throat, and his gaze shot to her eyes that held so much mischief.

"Any day now, Mr. Grumpy."

Harrison snorted at the name and slid his briefs down his legs. When he looked up, Nyla was at the edge of the bed, and she reached for him.

She wrapped her hand around his erection and began sliding it up and down his length rhythmically, and he groaned. He loved the way she stroked and fondled him, but when her thumb brushed across the tip of his dick, he almost lost it.

His hand shot out to grab the headboard, and his eyes slammed as a surge of pleasure charged through his body. Yeah, going slow was out of the question.

"Nyla. Baby," he said through gritted teeth and covered her hand with his. "That feels too damn good, and I'm close to losing control."

"Maybe I want you to lose control," she said, a wicked gleam in her eyes.

"Vixen," he said as he eased out of her grip before he embarrassed himself. He gave her a quick kiss, then yanked open his nightstand to pull out a couple of condoms. He tossed them aside before joining her on the bed.

His gaze roamed over her body, and he swallowed hard. She looked so beautiful.

"I already thought you were stunning, but this body? *Exquisite.*"

She laughed and started to say something, but Harrison didn't give her a chance. He crushed his mouth to hers and kissed her with a hunger he could barely control.

As their tongues tangled, he slid his hand down the side of her shapely body, squeezing and familiarizing himself with every dip and curve.

Before they were done, he planned to know every inch of her body.

He moved his mouth from hers and showered kisses over her cheek, near her ear, and worked his way to her graceful neck. Her skin was so soft, and she smelled like vanilla and heaven, and it all just made him want her that much more.

When he reached her breasts and cupped them within his palms, he and Nyla both moaned. God, this body. This breathtakingly, sexy, curvy body was all his right now, and he planned to enjoy himself while also bringing her extreme pleasure.

Harrison squeezed her breasts together and sucked a pert nipple into his mouth, feasting on it while Nyla squirmed beneath him. He split his time between both nipples, teasing the dark peaks until he had Nyla whimpering his name. The erotic sounds she made with every lap of his tongue was like music to his ears.

As his tongue continued exploring her breasts, he slowly slid a hand over her flat stomach, and he didn't stop until he reached the V between her legs.

"You're so wet," he mumbled against her skin as he glided a finger into her sweet heat and then added another.

"*Ohhh*," she breathed, and her back arched while her thighs closed around his hand, holding him in place. "Harrison," she whined as her hips moved up and down on their own accord while she humped his hand.

With each stroke of his fingers, he went deeper, and her moans grew louder. But when she started whimpering and tightening around his digits, Harrison picked up speed. He watched her as she got closer to her release. She looked so damn sexy, his dick throbbed with need. He couldn't wait to be inside her.

"Come for me, baby."

"I can't. I... Oh, my God! *Harrison!*" she screamed and

bucked against him, her body twisting back and forth as she screamed his name again.

"Oh! Oh, my goodness," Nyla whispered, her chest heaving as she struggled to get air into her lungs.

Her body jerked a few times as one aftershock after another shook her to her core. No man had ever made her lose control that quickly, and she could honestly say that Harrison had literally rocked her world.

Her breathing still wasn't back to normal when he leaned over her and kissed her with so much passion, she could've cried. Man, he was hitting her right in the heart with his tenderness.

He lifted his head slightly. "You're even more beautiful when you come," he crooned, and it was as soothing as a lullaby. When her lids started to droop, he kissed her again. "Stay with me," he said, as if she could actually go anywhere. Her body was like a limp noodle. She couldn't move.

A ghost of a smile played around his sexy lips when her eyes were finally able to focus on him. Had she said that out loud? She wasn't sure, but she was suddenly distracted when he opened the condom and sheathed his magnificent dick.

The man was hung like a damn horse. Thick. Long. Impressive. That was the only way to describe the equipment he was working with. And just like that, a flare of excitement charged through her, and suddenly, her whole being flooded with need.

Harrison moved his large body between her thighs and hovered above her before he lowered his head and covered her lips with his.

Nyla moaned into his mouth and wrapped her arms around his neck. He was such a good kisser. And he continued kissing her as he slid between her slick folds, inch by inch, stretching her until he was snug inside her.

He was so big, and he felt unbelievable as her body adjusted to his size.

As he began rocking his hips, he pulled his mouth from hers and his lips grazed the sensitive area beneath her ear. Just that quickly, he had found one of her erogenous zones. One that had the ability to make her lose control faster than she'd prefer.

Then he picked up speed, and Nyla gripped his arms to hold on as he went deeper and harder with each thrust. Pressure started swirling inside of her, and her nails dug into his skin as she moved in perfect sync with him.

"Damn, you feel incredible." His voice sounded strained as he started driving into her even faster, and his groans grew louder.

"Harrison... I'm about to come," Nyla whimpered, then cried out when pleasure rocketed through her, and her body tightened around him as she lost control. "*Ohmigod, Ohmigod.*" Her eyes slammed shut and her head thrashed back and forth against the pillow as she rode out her orgasm.

Harrison didn't stop. He kept thrusting until he growled his release and collapsed on top of her. Still trembling from aftershocks, Nyla held him close as he twitched a few times before his body settled down.

"Man," he wheezed, his heart beating hard against her chest. As if suddenly realizing he was lying on top of her, he lifted and rolled onto his back keeping a hand on her thigh. "You okay?" he asked, his voice thick and sounding sexy as his chest continued heaving.

"I'm wonderful," she panted.

They lay there for a moment, both out of breath until Harrison leaned over and kissed her. "You're amazing."

She gave him a tired smile. "Back at you, babe."

A few minutes later, Nyla watched as he went to the bathroom to take care of the condom. She must've dosed off at some point because, the next thing she knew, he was wrapping his arm around her.

She released a satisfied sigh and snuggled against his hard body.

That was mind-blowing was her last thought before she drifted off to sleep.

Chapter Seventeen

After a quick shower, Harrison changed into a pair of lounging pants and a long-sleeved T-shirt. After two rounds, Nyla had worn him out, and he couldn't stop the stupid grin from spreading across his face.

His little cutie-pie was full of surprises. First with the snowball fight and then their love making. Damn... it had been intense. He had fantasized about what they'd be like in bed together. Yet, what they'd shared for the last couple of hours exceeded anything he could've imagined. Sex with her had been the best he'd had in his life, and if he wasn't so tired and hungry, he'd convince her to go another round.

Later. They'd have a repeat later, but right now, he needed to feed his baby.

My baby.

The endearment, even in his head, felt right. They hadn't officially agreed to date, but as far as Harrison was concerned, Nyla was his. That alone spoke volumes about the type of person she was because it had been years since he'd wanted to claim a woman as his own. She was everything he could've wanted and more. Kind, sweet, gentle, thoughtful, funny, and the list could go on and on. Yeah, he needed to lock this down before the end of the weekend.

When he finally left the bathroom, Nyla was walking into the bedroom carrying a large tray loaded with food.

"Whoa, baby," Harrison hurried to her and carefully grabbed the tray. "This thing is heavy. Why didn't you ask me to bring it upstairs for you?"

Nyla shook out her arms and released a small laugh. "Well, when I came up with this brilliant idea of us eating in bed, I hadn't counted on the tray weighing a ton. Once I started up the stairs, I had to keep going."

Harrison set the tray in the middle of the bed, then turned to Nyla who was still shaking out her arms. He liked that she was making herself at home. She was even wearing one of his favorite T-shirts, his rattiest one. The one with Charlie Parker on the front of it playing his saxophone.

But the shirt looked hella good on her and stopped midthigh. It gave him a teasing view of her long, shapely legs, and if he wasn't mistaken, she wasn't wearing anything under it. Only one way to find out.

He tugged her into his arms and planted a kiss on her lips. "I like seeing you in my clothes," he mumbled against her mouth before lifting his head slightly. "You look good, taste good, and smell good. That's a lethal combination." His dick stirred as he nuzzled her neck while also cupping her firm butt cheeks.

He was right, she wasn't wearing a bra or panties. That knowledge spurred him on, and he kneaded her ass while pulling her flush against his body.

"If you don't stop, you're going to get something started, and though I wouldn't mind, I'm starving...*for food*," Nyla said on a moan.

Harrison chuckled and eventually loosened his hold on her. "I guess we did work up an appetite, but we're picking up where we left off after we eat."

"Deal!"

They moved to the bed and climbed on, each sitting on the opposite side of the tray.

Nyla grabbed a croissant that she had already sliced open and added mayo, Swiss cheese, and turkey. "I haven't eaten all day, and I think I can eat this whole spread by myself," she said around a mouthful of food.

Harrison had just reached for some strawberries but stopped and stared at her. "Why? I left breakfast for you."

"I know, and that was so sweet. Oh, and thank you for the beautiful roses! I can't believe I forgot to tell you that." She leaned over and gave him a quick kiss before she went back to devouring her sandwich.

"You're welcome," he said, loving the way her eyes lit up when she talked about him making her breakfast and buying her flowers. He wanted to give her the world if she'd let him.

"When I saw you outside shoveling, I immediately thought of having a snowball fight. I haven't had one since me and my siblings still lived at home."

She went on to talk about the shenanigans the five of them used to get into, including vicious snowball fights. Harrison smiled as she regaled him with one adventure after another of when they were teens. They were clearly a rambunctious bunch and were all only two or three years apart. He couldn't imagine how loud it must've been in their home.

As she continued talking, she grabbed a handful of grapes and popped one into her mouth. With the next one, she held the plump fruit to his lips. Harrison stared into her pretty brown eyes as he opened his mouth for her.

She smiled and while she slowly eased the fruit into his

mouth, he held her wrist steady and gently sucked on her fingers.

No woman had ever fed him before, and Harrison had to admit it was sexy as hell. Yeah, that was something else he wanted a repeat of. Nyla's smile turned wicked, and if that was any indication, feeding him was going to happen more often than not.

When she finally pulled her hand back, she shivered. "Stop distracting me so we can get back to the topic at hand. I need to teach you how to throw a snowball. You're either out of practice or never learned. Because what you were doing outside, shoving snow into my face, was *not* a snowball fight. Who does that anyway?"

He laughed at the way her eyebrows scrunched up and her lips twisted in mock disgust.

"Every male who has ever grown up with snow. That's who," Harrison said. "Snow was barely on the ground before me and my brother would charge outside to wrestle. At six years older than him, shoving the cold, white fluff into his face was my go-to move."

"I don't remember you ever talking about your siblings. How many do you have?"

"Two. A brother and a sister," he said, his chest tightening. Thinking about the fun he and his siblings used to have was suddenly overshadowed with memories he wasn't sure he wanted to revisit. "My brother, Geoffrey, is the youngest and my sister, Piper and I are three years apart."

"Tell me about them," Nyla said, and Harrison wasn't sure what she saw on his face, but she hurried to say, "If you'd rather not talk about—"

"No. I want you to know everything about me," he said, meaning it.

He'd held off long enough from talking about himself. Leaning back against the headboard, he stretched out his legs.

"When we were younger, both my parents worked full time. Meaning, I was left in charge often which was fine, mostly. My sister was never a problem. She was a peacemaker, always trying to keep everyone happy. She avoided anything that could lead to a confrontation. Even now, she's still like that, and she's one of my favorite people.

"My brother, on the other hand, drove me nuts." Harrison shook his head. "Yes, we had some fun despite the age difference, but he was the baby in the family, and my mother treated him as such. He could do no wrong. It didn't matter what he'd say or do or what type of trouble he got into, she'd defend him."

"Typical baby of the family," Nyla murmured.

"Yeah, but this baby of the family was a pain in the ass."

Nyla chuckled, and Harrison managed a small smile.

"It probably wouldn't have been so bad if my mother didn't undermine me when they'd leave me in charge. For as long as I can remember, she always made excuses for Geoffrey. Whether it was a fight at school or even him not doing his chores, she always justified his behavior. She'd say something like, *I'm sure he had a good reason.* Or *I'm sure he didn't mean it.* Or this or that. It got ridiculous.

"Parents usually say they don't have favorites, but it was always clear in our household that Geoffrey was her favorite. I only had a problem with that when she defended him and knew he was in the wrong. It got worse after my father died."

"Oh, my goodness, Harrison. I'm so sorry." Nyla moved the tray out the way and sat next to him, their bodies touching from hip to ankle. She reached for his hand and squeezed. "I didn't realize you'd lost your father."

He brought her hand to his lips and kissed the back of her knuckles.

"He had a heart attack at work when I was fifteen. He was the best. He's the one who fed into my love of music. It's because of him that I learned to play the sax and took piano, as well as guitar lessons."

Thinking about his father stirred mixed emotions. Harrison missed him like crazy, but he was thankful for the time they'd had together. As he shared stories about him with Nyla, some of the heaviness on his heart eased. Harrison Sr. was an all-around nice guy who loved his family and always made time for his kids.

"He sounds like a wonderful man."

Harrison nodded. "He was the best. It was tough after he died, but my mother did the best she could raising us. After graduating from high school, I moved out and attended the University of Chicago. A few years later, my sister did the same, but she went to school out of state. That left Geoffrey with my mother."

There'd been a time when Harrison felt guilty for not living at home while attending college. He hadn't liked leaving his mother only a couple of years after his father died, knowing how much she was missing his dad. But his mom assured him that she was fine, and she'd wanted him to have the college experience.

For Harrison, living near campus had been the best decision. He worked part time while attending college full time on a scholarship. Saving most of the money he'd earned, set him up well for after graduation.

"What about your sister?"

"She graduated from high school, then attended college in California. My mother was left with Geoffrey who'd started getting into trouble. Nothing major, but enough for me to keep my distance from both. At least until Geoffrey moved to Wisconsin for college and stayed there after graduation."

"Does your sister still live in California?"

Harrison shook his head. "Nah, she moved back a couple of years ago. She's a dentist and lives in Naperville."

Silence fell between them while Harrison tried to force his mouth to keep working. He trusted Nyla. Trusted her more than he'd trusted another woman in a long time. Still, a small part of him was hesitant to share more. Specifically, his painful past.

He reached over and turned on the Bluetooth speaker that was on his nightstand, and the sounds of Coltrane filled the room. Jazz music relaxed him. He glanced at Nyla and his heart leaped when she smiled. Even without makeup, her gorgeous face was still flawless.

"It's been awhile since I've listened to Coltrane. Good choice, he's one of my favorites," she said and laid her head on Harrison's shoulder.

"Mine too," he said as he rested his head against the cloth headboard. "I need to tell you something. Remember when I said I spent time in prison for a crime I didn't commit?"

Nyla stiffened next to him but then relaxed, and after a slight hesitation, she said, "Yeah." Stretching out the word.

"Well, what I didn't tell you was that my brother framed me for a murder he committed."

Chapter Eighteen

"What?" Nyla shouted, staring at him as if seeing him for the first time.

Harrison nodded. "Okay, maybe he didn't technically frame me, but he let me take the fall for the murder. He killed an elderly woman, and intentionally or unintentionally, made it look as if I'd done it. I was convicted of first-degree murder."

Nyla lifted her hands out in front of her, still looking a bit shell-shocked. "Wait. I—I... What. The. Hell! Are you kidding me? *Please* tell me your own brother didn't do what you're saying he did."

Harrison sighed. "I wish I could. Come here," he said, reaching for her.

He pulled her to his side and wrapped his arm around her shoulders. Having her close was as calming as the soft jazz flowing through the speaker.

"I'm not even sure where to start. It's a long story, baby, but I'll try to give you the Cliff's Notes version. I'm not going to lie, but this is hard to talk about."

She lifted her head and looked at him. "You can trust me," she said quietly. "Whatever we discuss in here, stays in here."

"I appreciate that, and by the time I'm done, you'll have a better understanding of why I struggle with trusting people." He rubbed his forehead, debating on where to start. "I bought this house for Veronica and me a little over five years ago. She never lived here, mainly because it needed a lot of renovation and, well, because she broke off our engagement.

"At any rate, my plan was to live here throughout the renovations, but it got impossible. There were construction workers in and out every day for weeks. That, along with all the noise and dust, had me going nuts. Between the renovations and wedding plans, that I didn't agree with, it was a lot.

"Which was why I didn't want to move in with Veronica. I couldn't listen to her wedding planning ideas twenty-four-seven. Which should've been my first sign that we weren't meant to be. At any rate, my mother suggested I stay at her house. She has four bedrooms and was always trying to get me and my siblings to visit more. I figured that would be the perfect time. She lives in the suburbs, but I could work from anywhere.

"After a couple of days of being at her place, my brother showed up. He lived in Kenosha with his girlfriend only a couple of hours away. It was also his winter break. So, it wasn't uncommon for him to visit my mother during that time. Problem was, like I mentioned before, he and I didn't mesh well. As adults, we tolerated each other, but you wouldn't find us out together having a beer."

"Did you know he was coming?"

"No, I didn't, and I considered leaving, but for the first few days, it was fine. Eventually though, we got into it. Actually, he was even being an ass to my mother. She'd tell him to clean up after himself, and he'd get all upset."

Harrison rubbed his chest as if that would loosen the unease swirling inside of him. For years, he'd worked hard to bury the memories of that time in his life, but talking about it was stirring it all up again.

He startled when Nyla touched his hand.

"If you need to stop, I—"

"No, I'm all right. I'm not sure if I'm recapping everything in order, but—"

"Just tell me what you want me to know," she said softly, and he was pretty sure he fell a little harder for her in that moment.

He had once told himself that he was done with women. That he didn't need one in his life, but in the months of getting to know Nyla, she had changed all that. She had fallen into his life by chance, and though he didn't believe in fate, he was starting to.

"I thought maybe there was something else going on with Geoffrey that he hadn't told us," Harrison continued. "When I tried talking to him, asking a few questions, he told me to mind my own business. Said that with my perfect life I wouldn't understand, and then he left. He told my mother that he was going home to talk with his girlfriend. But the day after that, my mother came to me and suggested I return home."

"What?" Nyla glanced at him. "She asked *you* to leave?"

Harrison nodded. "She said Geoffrey had come for a visit because he'd had a fight with his woman. Arriving at our mother's house was supposed to give him some peace and give him a chance to regroup. Even though he had left to return to Kenosha, she told me that he was planning to return to her house, but he might not if I was still there."

Harrison's pulse pounded loudly in his ear, and he closed his eyes, willing himself to relax. He sucked in a lung full of air and released it slowly. All the while, Nyla remained quiet.

"I couldn't..." he started but stopped and rubbed his forehead as sadness suddenly gripped him. No way was he going to break down. Not now. Not in front of the woman he was quickly beginning to care about.

"I couldn't believe she was kicking me out. *My own mother*. It wasn't like I couldn't go home, but it was the principle of it. I didn't bother reminding her that I was the one who'd gifted her the majority of the money to buy that house. Instead, I packed my shit and got the hell out of there."

"It's no wonder you never want to talk to her at work. I don't blame you."

"Actually, that's not even the reason I cut ties with her. She did something else that I can't forget or forgive. I'll tell you about it but let me keep going with this part of the story."

"Okay."

"For days after I left her house, I took my frustrations out on a punching bag at the gym. I knew I shouldn't have been surprised at how things turned out. That's how it always was when it came to Geoffrey and my mother. He had always been her golden child. Still, I'd been devastated."

He'd been more than devastated. He'd been furious, and those feelings from all those years ago came rushing back. His pulse pounded and his chest heaved despite him trying to keep himself together.

He scrubbed his hands down his face, determined to keep talking, but it was hard. It was hard to tell anyone about one of the most humiliating days in his life.

Nyla glanced up at him. "Harrison?"

"Umm...sorry. I umm... A few days after all that happened, the cops showed up at my job. Didn't give a damn who was around when they told me I was under arrest for the murder of Mildred Robinson."

* * *

Nyla tried not to react, but she was sure her face showed her anger and her shock. Weeks ago, when he'd mentioned going to prison for a murder he hadn't committed, she hadn't known what to expect. But this? This was some next level dysfunctional family soap opera shit that you see on TV. No way was this his life.

Her heart broke for Harrison, for all that he'd endured. He must've been terrified. Having your freedom snatched away in the blink of an eye and being tossed in jail was beyond scary.

Questions whirled through her mind, but she wasn't sure what to ask first. Instead, she remained quiet, barely, and hoped he'd keep talking.

"The neighbor, Miss Robinson, was found beaten to death in her backyard. She had also been robbed. According to them, she had just returned from grocery shopping when she'd been attacked. The bags of food were scattered around her."

"Surely the cops didn't think you did this."

"They did. When they took me to the station for questioning, they showed me a grainy video of me talking to Miss Robinson at her front door. I remember that day because her packages had been delivered to my mother's house, and I dropped them off. I was over there a few times. Shoveling snow, picking up baked goods that she'd made for us, and I even moved a bookshelf to her basement. I had also replaced a storm window at the back of her house.

"So yeah, I had been there often. I'm not sure if cameras caught each of those visits, but the detective showed me a video of a guy running out of the backyard. They also had turned part of the video into photos, trying to capture the man's...or my brother's face. Nyla, when I was watching that video, if I didn't know it wasn't me, I would've thought it was. Same build, coat, boots, everything, but neither video nor photos showed the man's face."

"At any time, did you think it was your brother?"

"*No. Not at all.* It hadn't crossed my mind. Geoffrey was a lot of things, but I *never* thought he was capable of murder. All I knew was that I hadn't killed that woman."

Nyla was numb. It was bad enough knowing that someone would harm an elderly woman, but to know that someone was Harrison's brother? She shook her head, still processing his story. It was no wonder he'd been standoffish when they'd met. Or that Jamie had said Harrison had trust issues. This type of experience would change anyone.

Harrison continued. At the time of the murder, he'd been home. Unfortunately, no one could vouch for his whereabouts. Some of his mother's neighbors told the cops that the guy in the photos looked like him. They remembered his coat. They had also seen him talking to Miss Robinson almost every day.

More tears pricked Nyla's eyes as he told her about all the evidence they'd collected against him. Evidence that made it look like he'd been the murderer. They had searched his house and destroyed some of the renovations that had been done. All the while Harrison had maintained his innocence.

They'd found blood on the front of his coat that matched the victim. They hadn't believed him when he told them it wasn't what they thought. Days before her death, Miss Robinson had accidentally touched his coat before realizing she had cut her finger after chopping vegetables. Nobody believed him.

His boots were also evidence. They'd had the same tread as a boot print found in the backyard. It also hadn't helped Harrison's case that his knuckles had been bruised from all the boxing he'd done before his arrest. They claimed it was from beating up Miss Robinson.

"I was mentally and emotionally lost. Veronica had hired a lawyer for me, someone her family knew," Harrison said of his ex-fiancée. "At the time, I couldn't remember if the guy ever asked me if I had killed the woman. I didn't even know if the man who was supposed to be representing me, *defending* me, believed that I was innocent.

"Those first few months, I think I was in a daze. So much I still don't remember, especially about the trial. My therapist said I might've blocked it out. I don't know. There'd been so much that had happened that I didn't have the mental ability to deal with it."

"My God," Nyla whispered.

Harrison rubbed a hand over his mouth, and Nyla didn't miss the tears in his eyes. They didn't fall, but they were there.

"The wheels of justice turn so slow, and not getting bail kept me behind bars well before my trial. Then after hearing the evidence, the jury found me guilty. They tossed my ass in prison and didn't give a damn that I maintained I was innocent."

Nyla feverishly swiped at her tears. She wanted to say something, but she feared if she did, she'd burst out crying. Instead, she wrapped her arms around Harrison's waist and held on tightly.

"If it hadn't been for Royce, I don't know where I'd be right now. He kept my life intact on the outside. My job was saved. My mortgage was paid, and... Let's just say, I owe him my life. I owe him everything."

Nyla listened as he recounted how his boss, Royce, had vowed that they were going to prove his innocence. They weren't sure if Harrison's first lawyer or the cops had done due diligence when it came to investigating. Royce got him a new lawyer and within weeks, Harrison's case was reopened. Thanks to a private investigator, they'd learned that some of the witnesses had been coerced into a statement. At the time, Harrison didn't know whether his first lawyer had talked to his mother, Geoffrey, or Geoffrey's girlfriend, but the P.I. of his second lawyer had.

"All the details began falling into place. Geoffrey's girlfriend had lied, saying that he'd been with her in Kenosha during the time of the murder. I still don't know exactly how they found this out, but Geoffrey had a coat identical to mine."

"What?"

Harrison nodded. "My coat had been a Christmas present from my mother the year before I got arrested. I had no idea she had also bought the same coat for my brother."

"*Oh. My. God.* You're not saying..."

Nyla's words trailed off, and Harrison couldn't seem to speak for a moment.

Seconds ticked by before he said, "When it came out that my mother knew it could've been Geoffrey in those photos, and she never said anything, it had been the ultimate betrayal. She had eventually admitted to fearing that it was Geoffrey, but she'd said she couldn't believe he would do something like that."

The more Harrison talked, Nyla could feel the tension in his body ratcheting, and though she was glad he was sharing, she hated she had him reliving this horrible time in his life. She kept her head on his chest and gently rubbed her hand in circular motions over his flat stomach.

But when his body started shaking, she bolted upright and found him silently crying.

God...

Not knowing what else to do, she straddled his lap and wrapped her arms around his neck, glad that he wrapped his around her too. They both cried. She didn't know how long they stayed that way, but eventually Harrison kissed the side of her forehead, then loosened his grip on her.

"I'm sorry," he said. "I knew talking about this would be hard, but I didn't know I'd get this emotional."

Nyla gently gripped his face between her hands, forcing him to look at her. "You have nothing to apologize for. Sweetheart, I am so sorry you had to go through all this. It's no wonder you want nothing to do with your mother."

He released a ragged sigh. "I was emotionally destroyed, and it took *years* to close the gaping hole in my heart." He chuckled and shook his head. "I can't believe that just came out of my mouth. Sounds like a damn country song."

Still holding his face between her hands, Nyla chuckled and caressed his damp cheek with the pad of her thumb. "I thought it sounded poetic." She kissed him slowly before climbing off his lap and resting her head on his broad shoulder.

After a long hesitation, Harrison continued. "I haven't talked to Geoffrey since before that day my mother kicked me out of her house. Nor did I attend his trial. I heard he was charged with second-degree murder and is set to serve twenty-five years in prison.

"Supposedly, he hadn't intended to kill Miss Robinson. He had just planned to rob her. Which isn't any better. But she surprised him by fighting back, and he accidentally shoved her too hard. She hit her head on the back of the house. Supposedly, he'd lost his job and needed money."

Nyla closed her eyes, fighting another wave of tears. Senseless. It was like people didn't value life anymore. Another senseless death.

"Why do you think your mother has been calling?"

"I'm not completely sure. She called me last month on Christmas, which is normal, but she normally doesn't call this often."

"Maybe something's happened. Have you talked to your sister?"

"Yeah, I talked to Piper this morning while you were asleep. We made an agreement years ago that whenever she and I talk, she can't mention our mother. I know it sounds crazy, but my sister is a peacemaker. If it was left up to her, we'd all be one big happy, yet dysfunctional family living under the same roof. Though she hates what my mother did to me, she can't abandon her, which I didn't expect her to."

Harrison grew quiet, and Nyla waited for him to continue.

"This morning, for the first time, Piper said I should talk to our mother. I didn't ask why, and she didn't say. So, I assume something's going on, but I don't want to talk to her.

"I know they say forgiveness improves your health and helps reduce stress. Hopefully, I'll be able to forgive her someday, but I'm not there yet."

Nyla believed in forgiveness, but what his mother did was unconscionable. If Nyla were Harrison, she wasn't sure she'd be able to forgive and move on either. But she wanted to do whatever she could to help him get the closure he needed.

"The main two women in my life at that time, the ones who claimed to love me, the ones who I thought I could always count on, let me down."

Nyla shook her head. Who were these people who hadn't loved Harrison enough to stand by him? To believe in him? To help him get his freedom? She hoped she never ran into either woman. She might do something crazy like haul off and punch them. Which would make her just as bad as them.

"Veronica's family own a ton of businesses, one being a local gossip newspaper. After I was released from prison, and my record cleared, they wanted my story. Veronica didn't work there, but her father pressured her to try to get an exclusive."

"You gotta be kidding me," Nyla said, disgust dripping from each word.

"Nope, and I made it clear that I wouldn't be giving an interview to anyone. For weeks, I was hounded by the media. I couldn't leave my home, not that I wanted to, but every local network wanted my story."

That probably had a lot to do with why he hadn't returned to playing in nightclubs. He was so musically gifted, but he probably feared the media would come back around.

Nyla wasn't a big TV watcher, and she had never heard Harrison's story before today. Though she'd been tempted to google him a couple of weeks ago, she was glad she hadn't. Letting him tell *his* story instead of reading what the media had to say about it was better.

"It was horrible having cameras and microphones shoved into my face. It got so bad I worked from home for a while and barely went out in public."

"I hate you went through all this."

"Yeah, which was why I had no choice but to see a therapist after being released. I didn't know what to do with the anxiety, the depression, and the feeling of loss. I met with her for a year, and then I started back not long ago once I was ready to really get my life on track. I don't go weekly like I used to, but even every few months for check-ins have been helpful."

When he yawned and slumped down a bit farther in the bed, Nyla knew it was time to let him get some rest.

She sat up. "Why don't you take a nap. You were up late last night, and I know you got up early this morning. You must be tired."

Harrison wrapped his arm around her and kissed the side of her forehead. "I am, but I need you to know how much I appreciate you listening to me. I know that was a lot to share, but talking with you really helped. I feel more at peace. So thank you."

She kissed his lips. "Anytime and thank you for trusting me. I know that wasn't easy for you. Now, how about you get some sleep?"

"I'll only take a nap if you stay in here with me."

Nyla grinned up at him. "Okay, but we're going to *sleep*. No funny stuff, Mr."

He laughed and her heart leaped. God, it sounded good to hear him laugh. After hearing his story, it was amazing he still could.

Harrison rolled her onto her back and hovered above her. He kissed her slowly and sweetly. "How about we take a short nap and then play around?"

Nyla rolled her eyes playfully and sighed dramatically. "*Fine*. Whatever you want."

Chapter Nineteen

The weekend went by too fast, Harrison thought as he stared out the kitchen window drinking a cup of coffee. It was Sunday, late morning, and according to Nyla, time for her to get back to her life. If he had his way, she would be by his side forever, and wasn't that funny?

He grunted and shook his head. For years, and even as recent as weeks, he had vowed that he'd never let a woman get close to his heart again. And wasn't he the one who vowed to be a bachelor until he took his last breath?

That would be a yes, but that was before Nyla came into his life. He had never fallen for a woman as quickly as he'd fallen for her. Surprisingly, it didn't freak him out. If anything, he was more at peace today than he'd been in the last five years. Happier too, and he owed it all to Nyla Priestly.

"What are you thinking about?" Nyla asked as she looped her arms around his waist from behind. Her hands rested on his stomach, and he covered them with his free hand and squeezed.

"You," he said simply. "I was thinking about how sensational you are, and how I've enjoyed having you here."

Even though yesterday's conversation about his past had worn him out, after a nap, he felt refreshed. It was as if talking to Nyla about his life helped him release the burden of keeping that information to himself.

The year he'd been arrested had been the worst year of his life. A year plagued with hurt, betrayal, humiliation, and loss. Yet he survived it. That was something Nyla made him see last night when they'd continued the conversation over dinner. No, he would never want to relive that time but surviving it had made him stronger. After what he went through, he could now handle anything that life threw his way.

Harrison sat his mug on the counter and turned within Nyla's hold until he was facing her. Bending down, he captured her mouth with his. He loved kissing her, holding her, and inhaling her essence. She felt like a gift that he hadn't known he needed or wanted, and he would cherish her for as long as she'd have him.

When the kiss ended, he asked. "What are your plans for the rest of the day?"

Nyla sucked in air and released it slowly as she moved out of his hold. "That's a good question. At first, I was going to have you drive me home. However, if you don't mind, can you drop me off at my parents' B & B instead? It'll give me a chance to visit with them for a minute. Then my father and I are going to look at a car that a friend of his is selling. I didn't want to spend the money on one yet, but I need a vehicle."

"I would let you use my other car, but it's not great in this type of weather," he said of his older model BMW. It was in immaculate condition, but he learned the hard way that it wasn't good in snow.

Nyla moved around the center island and sat on one of the

Believing in You

barstools. "That's sweet of you, but I need to do this for more reasons than just needing transportation."

Harrison frowned. "What other reason is there?"

She lowered her gaze and nibbled on her lower lip. "A couple of weeks ago, my sister, Cree, told me that I needed to grow up. I've been couch surfing, bumming rides, and basically not standing on my own two feet."

"Do you need money?" Harrison asked, prepared to do anything that could help her.

"I have the money to support myself, but it's earmarked for buying Moody Days. I need to prove, mainly to myself, that I can afford to support myself while also buying and owning a business."

Harrison leaned on the counter in front of her. "I see. Can you?"

"It's going to be tight, especially since I don't know if I'll have enough saved by the time Gordon retires in a couple of months. Even though I hadn't wanted to hear it, Cree was right. I need to get my priorities straight. I have to have a roof over my head and dependable transportation."

Harrison wanted to suggest she move in with him, but that wouldn't be helpful. Clearly, these changes were something she needed to prove to herself. Even if he'd love to have her under his roof every day for the rest of their lives.

"Would you consider an investor or a silent partner for Moody Days?"

"No," she said quickly, a sting behind that one word. "I don't want anyone telling me how to run a business that I've been managing for years. That's exactly what would happen if they got involved."

Her words were spoken with passion and maybe even a little anger. It was safe to say this was a sore subject.

"Why not?" he asked carefully. "Why wouldn't you want to hear their opinions or suggestions?"

"Because I know what I'm doing!" she snapped, fire in her eyes. "Just because they all have college degrees doesn't mean they know better than I do. I know how to run that club. I don't need them telling me what to do!"

Harrison lifted his hands. "Okay. Okay, I get it. You've already proven that you can run the club. Nobody—especially not me—is denying that. I'm sorry. I'm sure if they offered you money to help you achieve your dream of business ownership, it wasn't because they didn't believe in you."

She blew out a breath and glanced away. "No, I'm the one who's sorry. I keep letting my insecurities make me lash out. I know you mean well, but Harrison I have to do this myself."

Their conversation the other night came to mind. He'd forgotten that she felt inferior to those with college degrees. If only she could see herself the way he saw her. Strong, smart, intuitive. He'd seen those qualities in her the first week she worked at Telecom. She handled every assignment given to her with ease and professionalism. There was no doubt that others saw those qualities in her too, and that's what he told her.

Moving around the counter, he sat next to her. "You're an amazing woman who can accomplish anything you set out to do. I'm sure I speak for me and your family when I say that."

"Thank you." She squeezed his arm. "I appreciate you saying that. I know my insecurities are in my head, but occasionally, they make an appearance when I least expect it."

"That happens to all of us from time to time. I'm just glad you haven't let that stop you from pursuing your dreams. Would you consider a silent investor?"

She narrowed her eyes at him, but when she opened her mouth to probably say no, he lifted his hands to silence her.

"Hear me out before you automatically shoot down my

idea. After releasing me from prison, the state gave me fifty-thousand-dollars."

Her mouth dropped open. "Seriously?"

He nodded. As far as he was concerned, they owed him a helluva lot more than that, but he kept that to himself.

"I lost a year of my life, and I guess that was their way of saying sorry, let us help you out. Anyway, I invested the money in stocks that have done extremely well. I haven't touched the funds because I've been wanting to invest in a business. Why not Moody Days? Let me help you obtain your dream."

Nyla started shaking her head before he could finish the last sentence, but he pushed on.

"I can have a contract drawn up that says that I'm only an investor. I won't have any say in how you run the business. All decisions are your own unless you ask my opinion on something. You won't have to pay interest or anything back for the first five years that you're in business."

"Harrison…"

"It'll all be in writing. Whether you and I make it as a couple or not, and yes, we're a couple," he added quickly, "the money is yours for five years with three percent interest. After the five-year mark, you'll start paying it back in monthly installments."

"Harrison, I can't ask you to do that."

"You didn't ask. I'm offering."

She was still shaking her head. "That's a horrible investment. You wouldn't be receiving much of a return, especially with that low interest rate."

"I've been planning to find a business to invest in, and I can't think of a better one than Moody Days. If it makes you feel better, we can negotiate a deal. At any rate, my love for jazz and music is only part of the reason why I think this is a good idea. The other? Not only will I be investing in your business, but I'll be investing in you. *Baby, I believe in you.* I know you can make the club even more successful than you already have."

Tears filled her eyes, and his heart lurched. The last thing he wanted to do was make her cry, even if they were happy tears.

"If you cry, you might make me cry, and I did enough of that yesterday."

She laughed, but he was serious. He had never cried in front of a woman, and he never wanted to again. Hell, the only time he could ever remember shedding tears was that first night in prison after the jury found him guilty. He had lost hope and thought his life was over. He had also cried when his father died, but that didn't count since he'd been a child at the time.

"I don't know what to say," Nyla whispered.

Harrison stood and stretched out his hand. "Say we have a deal or that we'll start working on a deal."

She looked at his hand for a second before sliding her smaller one into his grasp. They shook hands, and Harrison gently tugged her to him.

"I really do believe in you, and I'm glad you're going to let me help you make your dream come true."

"I don't know how I'll ever be able to thank you," she said, putting her arms around his neck.

"You can thank me by being the best damn club owner in Chicago."

She grinned at him and heat spread to every cell in his body. His new life mission was to keep that smile on her gorgeous face.

Harrison kissed her long and hard, savoring her unique, sweet taste. He regretted that their weekend was coming to an end, but he was happier than he'd been in a long time. She made him feel alive again.

"I wish I could keep you here forever," he mumbled against her lips before pulling back.

Nyla glanced up at him. "The feeling is mutual, and though that would be fun, it's not realistic."

Maybe not yet but one day, Harrison wanted to say but kept the thought to himself. What he didn't want to do was move too fast and scare her away. Yet, he believed with all his heart she was the one for him. His other half. The person who completed him. The person who he would spend the rest of his life with.

It was only a matter of time.

Chapter Twenty

Nyla stared out the window of Harrison's SUV replaying their earlier conversation through her mind.

I believe in you.

His words played around in her head, and she smiled to herself. He always seemed to know the perfect thing to say, and she had needed to hear those words.

During her shower that morning, she had made the decision that she'd be moving out of Cree's place in the next week or two. Unless she found an apartment sooner. In deciding that, she had also planned to talk to Gordon and ask if he could give her a few more months.

But then Harrison came along and made her an offer she didn't want to refuse. The timing couldn't have been better. Even if she had some reservations about mixing business with pleasure, she couldn't deny that he was making her an offer of a lifetime.

A silent investor. Not a silent partner. That was something she could get with. She just hoped he didn't change his mind, though she didn't think he would. He was ready to get it all on paper whenever she was available.

It was the end of January, if she and Harrison could finalize the details of the contract over the next few days, she could own Moody Days before the end of February. Then she and Gordon would get what they wanted. She'd be a business owner, and he'd get to finally retire.

Harrison pulled in front of the walkway that ran along the side of the B & B that led to her parents' cottage and parked.

"I still don't want to let you go," he said, pushing his black-rimmed glasses up on his nose.

For most of the weekend, he'd worn contacts, but this morning, she was surprised to see that his glasses were back. He was handsome either way. As long as she could still gaze into his intense, almond-shaped eyes, he could wear whichever he wanted.

"Two days with you aren't enough."

"I know." Nyla tried keeping the whine out of her voice but failed. She wasn't ready to say goodbye either. She undid her seatbelt and leaned over the center console. "This has been the best weekend ever. Thanks for coming to my rescue Friday. Thanks for making me feel extra special Saturday and thank you for your business offer this morning."

"All of that was my pleasure," he said and ran the back of his fingers gently down her cheek. "I should be thanking you again because I feel freer than I have felt in a very long time. I feel like a new man. I know that has everything to do with spending time with you, as well as our talk yesterday."

Harrison cupped her cheek and stared into her eyes, and Nyla's heart thumped a little faster. It was too soon to call what she saw brimming in his dark orbs *love*, but she had no doubt that he cared deeply for her. The feeling was mutual if not a little scary.

His large hand slid to her chin and nudged her forward until her mouth was a breath from his. Nyla smiled. She couldn't help it. Giddiness swirled inside of her at his nearness, and the way he was still looking at her made her fall a little harder for him. Then, his lips met hers in a sweet, tender kiss that was as light as a summer breeze, and she moaned against his mouth.

No one had ever made her feel so cherished. One would think this was their first time making out, but of course it wasn't. Yet, each time her lips connected with his, he roused a passion within her that she hadn't known existed.

She wanted this. She wanted to always feel this sense of happiness that filled her whenever he kissed or touched her intimately. To think, she'd been with men who she thought she had loved, but no one ever made her feel this...complete.

When the kiss ended, Harrison touched his forehead to hers. "While we were talking earlier, I mentioned that you and I are a couple. I shouldn't have assumed, but Nyla, I want you in my life. I know we've only known each other a few months, but this feels right. *We* feel right."

Nyla knew she should say something, but the words didn't come. Instead, she pulled back and diverted her gaze as her pulse amped. She wanted to be with him more than anything, but all she kept thinking was that he was out of her league. Sure, he might still be working on himself emotionally, but in every other aspect of his life, he had his stuff together.

"Considering you look like you want to bolt, was I being too presumptuous in thinking we could be a couple?"

She glanced at him. "Harrison, you're a remarkable man and can have any woman you want. Why me?"

He frowned and his confused expression looked sincere. "Why not you? You're beautiful, smart, fun to be with, and more than anything, you make me smile. Which is something I haven't done much of in years, but when I'm with you, I feel... I feel exhilarated."

"I feel the same way," she said, her heart squeezing at the conviction in his words. "But I'm still trying to get my life together, and right now, I have nothing to offer you."

"Nyla, you have given me more in the last few months than I've received from anyone in years. You make me happy. You bring me joy. Do you know how valuable that is in the world we live in these days? I understand that you're putting your life in order while preparing to become a business owner, and I'll support you anyway I can. I'll also accept whatever time in your busy days that you can share with me. I just want you in my life."

She lowered her gaze and nibbled on her bottom lip. Normally, she was a risk taker, trying almost anything at least once. But when it came to matters of the heart, not so much. Especially after John dumped her for not being enough for him.

"What's this really about? What are you afraid of?"

"I'm afraid I'm going to fall in love with you, and then you're going to break my heart by telling me I'm not enough for you. That I'm not smart enough, or pretty enough, or hell, even tall enough. I can't handle another rejection like that."

He reached for her hand and brought it to his lips and kissed the back of her knuckles. "Whatever asshole told you that you weren't enough for him, didn't deserve you. Nyla, I'm not him. Maybe I want something different in my life from what he wanted. Besides, don't lump me into the same category as that jerk. I'm not going to hurt you. You already mean too much to me for that to happen."

She searched his eyes, hoping he was telling the truth. Butterflies took flight in her stomach and sent her spirits soaring at the idea of being Harrison's woman. Could she really be enough for him? And could she trust him with her heart?

"Yesterday, you told me that I can trust you, and I do. Now, I need you to trust me," he said as if reading her mind. "Will you be my woman?"

"Yes," she said, fighting an overwhelming desire to throw herself into his arms and hold on for dear life. "Yes. A thousand times, yes."

Despite the center console being in the way, Harrison hugged her tightly and kissed the side of her head.

"Thank you for taking a chance on me."

Just then, a car slowed and parked in front of them, and Nyla almost groaned when she realized it was Cree and their mother. She was fine with it being her sister, but her mother? Not so much.

She scurried out of Harrison's hold. "It's a good thing you suggested we date officially because I kinda told my mother I had a boyfriend."

His eyebrows shot up. "Oh really. Who was the lucky guy?"

"Actually, you. I figured since you saved me from the ladder at Telecom that day, you automatically became my man."

He laughed and like usual, the hearty sound warmed her. Though she didn't think she had time for a relationship, Nyla wanted more than anything to make theirs work. Not just because they both needed some fun in their lives, but Harrison was like a dream come true. He had all of Prince Charming's qualities and more.

She was definitely going to have to thank Jamie for insisting they get to know each other. But first, she needed to get through this day with her mother.

"That's my mother, Virginia Priestly, climbing out of the passenger side door," Nyla whispered as if her mother could hear her.

"I see where you get your good looks from. She's beautiful," Harrison said, his voice level matching hers.

They had apparently just come from church if her mother's wide rimmed, navy-blue hat was any indication. Her heavy cream-colored coat hid the outfit, but Nyla was sure it matched the hat, her purse, and her navy-blue high heel boots.

"I should warn you. My mother has been hounding me and my siblings for grandkids. Once you step out of this car, I won't be able to protect you."

Harrison grinned, then started laughing. "Surely, she can't be that bad."

Just then, her mother stopped in the middle of the sidewalk and stared at the SUV, as if waiting for them to get out.

This time, Nyla did groan. She wasn't ready to introduce Harrison to her family. Not that she was ashamed of him. No, it had everything to do with the fifty-million questions they might ask him. Especially her mother.

Nyla turned to Harrison. "She is that bad, and I'm being a hundred percent serious. She's been on this mission to get me and my siblings booed up, married, and pumping out babies soon after."

His grin dropped, and he glanced over Nyla's shoulder out the passenger window. After a few seconds, he waved at someone, and Nyla assumed her mother was still standing there.

"Well, you're already *booed* up," he said, looking at Nyla with roguishness in his eyes. "And I can totally get with marrying you and having you as my babies' momma." He climbed out of the SUV without a backwards glance.

Nyla sat frozen. They were barely dating. No way would she allow her mind to go there and envision a family with Harrison. It would be a dream come true, but that would be getting way ahead of herself.

When he opened her car door and extended his hand to

her, Nyla placed her hand in his. Her heart did a cartwheel inside her chest at what she saw in his heated gaze. Desire. Passion. Love.

If she wasn't already in love with this man, she was pretty damn close.

Chapter Twenty-One

Meeting members of Nyla's family hadn't been on his list of things to do today, but there was no time like the present.

"Mom, Cree, this is Harrison Grant. Harrison, this is my mother, Virginia, and my sister."

"Nice to meet you." He shook Cree's hand and then extended his hand to their mother.

"Oh, no, love. I don't shake hands. I'm a hugger. Bring it in," Virginia said, her arms outstretched with her purse dangling from one of them while her gloved fingers beckoned him to come closer.

He obliged, hugging her and almost laughing at how long she held on to him. But then it was as if a Mack truck slammed into him and knocked him off-balance when a sudden memory crashed into him. It was of his mother hugging him tightly. Tight enough for him to feel her love seeping into his veins.

Harrison swallowed hard, forcing himself not to leap out of Virginia's hold while remembering how his mother used to give the best hugs. His mind spun. His throat tightened, and his heart started beating double time.

What the hell?

He forced himself to remain calm. The memory was so random, but it felt as if he'd been transported back in time. He could almost see his mother's face and feel her arms around him.

When Virginia finally loosened her hold, Harrison tried to put some distance between them, but she didn't release him. Instead, she held him at arm's length with her hands on his shoulders.

She stared at him for what seemed like an hour but was only seconds before saying, "You have kind eyes." Her voice was barely loud enough for him to hear as she continued to search his eyes as if able to see deep into his soul. When she finally released him. He scurried backwards, trying not to be obvious about it but needing to put space between them.

Nyla was right there. She slipped her hand into his and squeezed. It was as if she knew something had transpired during that embrace. An embrace that shook him.

"You have to come inside and meet my husband," Virginia said as she slid her purse strap onto her shoulder and smiled at him. "Then you can have lunch with all of us."

"I—I appreciate that, Mrs. Priestly, but—"

"Mom, Harrison has things to do," Nyla said while gently rubbing his arm.

"Nonsense," Virginia said. "I'm sure he doesn't mind staying a little while to get to know us. Do you, Harrison?"

"Actually, I—"

"Come on, Love, you can spare an hour or so. Let's get out of this cold before we turn into icicles." She slid her arm through the crook of his as if it were the most natural thing to do. "Nice arms," she complimented, giving his biceps a little squeeze, and Harrison grunted.

Nyla had warned him, and Virginia was living up to her reputation of being... a lot.

He tightened his hold on Nyla's hand while she grumbled under her breath about pushy mothers. That didn't stop Virginia as she guided them up the walkway with a pep in her step. Harrison was fairly sure he heard Cree chuckling behind them, but he wasn't positive.

When they made it into the cottage, four sets of similar brown eyes turned in their direction.

"Hey family! This is Harrison, Nyla's boyfriend," Virginia announced happily before anyone could speak.

Then she pulled him away from Nyla and walked him farther into the living room. The family had been watching an NFL playoff game on a big screen television mounted on the wall. It was loud. The sound pumped through surround-sound speakers until someone turned down the volume.

"Harrison, this is my son, Zion, my oldest daughter, Essence, my grandson, Tray, and my incredibly handsome husband, Israel."

Her husband shook his head, seeming unfazed by his wife's words as he slowly stood.

"Hello, everyone," Harrison said, giving a small wave and feeling a little warm around the collar. He unzipped his coat, hoping that would help as Nyla's family greeted him.

"Virginia, let the boy at least take off his coat and boots before you start pulling him all around the house," Israel said as he approached.

"Okay, fine. Just don't let him leave until I have time to spend with him."

"Oh, Mom, don't start. Nyla doesn't need you scaring him

away before he gets to know the *sane* family members," Essence said and winked at Harrison.

"Harrison, you see how they treat me?" Virginia called out as Essence moved her down the hallway. "Anyway, we'll get food on the table as soon as I change out of my church clothes."

Virginia continued talking as she disappeared to the back of the house, and Harrison couldn't help but laugh. The woman was funny.

"Nice to meet you, son," Israel said, shaking Harrison's hand. "Sorry about my wife. She loves people. If you're dating one of our kids, Virginia has already adopted you as one of her own. So welcome. Let me take your coat and get you something to drink."

"Thanks, Dad, but I got it," Nyla said, ushering Harrison out of the room and back toward the foyer.

"Oh, my God! I'm so sorry," she whispered, sliding her arms inside his wool coat and around his waist before she looked up at him. "Are you okay? I told you my mom is a lot, but she means well."

Harrison hugged Nyla back, probably holding on a little too tightly as he breathed her in. Being in her arms was like a calming elixir, and his nerves immediately settled. He didn't want to let her go.

After a few minutes, Nyla pulled him closer to the front door and far enough away from the others where they wouldn't be heard. In the process, they took off their coats, and she hung them in the coat closet.

"You looked a bit shell-shocked outside. Are you okay?"

He didn't want to admit Virginia's embrace had shaken him to his core. He was still getting used to socializing, but he never had that reaction to anyone. Then again, he could already tell Virginia was like no other.

"Yeah, I'm fine," he said just above a whisper, but Nyla

didn't look convinced, so he told her. "Your mother's hug reminded me of my mother. Despite how things ended between us, she used to give the best hugs. I was caught off guard for a minute there, but it's all good."

"I'm so sorry, babe," she said, cupping his cheek as she stared into his eyes. "If you need to leave, I totally understand, but why don't you stick around and have lunch. I'll make sure I keep my mother away from you."

He chuckled and gave her a quick kiss. "I appreciate that, baby, but since we're dating, I need to get used to being around your family." And other people too, he wanted to add but didn't. So far, Nyla's family seemed as refreshing as she was.

"Excuse me. Sorry to interrupt."

Harrison turned to find Cree standing a few feet away.

"Harrison, have we met before? I don't usually forget a face, and you look very familiar."

"I saw you from a distance at Moody Days a week or two ago. Maybe that's where you remember me from," he said, though he didn't think so.

It was the same night he had learned that Nyla managed the jazz club. Cree and one of their other sisters were hugging Nyla before they left the club.

"Maybe, but..." She shrugged. "Anyway, I'll let you two get back to what you were doing," she said and strolled toward the kitchen.

When Harrison turned back to Nyla, she had a strange look on her face.

"What?" he said.

She moved closer and wrapped her arms around him again before whispering, "She's an entertainment lawyer, and she devours the news daily. What if..." Her voice trailed off, and he knew what she was thinking: *What if Cree knows what happened to you?*

When he decided to start living again, Harrison told himself that he was risking being recognized. Risking people talking about him behind his back or asking him questions about the worst time in his life.

No, deep down he wasn't ready for any of it. Yet, as he stared into Nyla's beautiful eyes, the only thing he knew for sure was that he wanted her in his life. If that meant her family knowing his history, that was a chance he had to take.

He bent down and nuzzled her neck just below her ear. "It's okay," he said and placed a kiss there. "I'm in this for the long haul. At some point, your family will find out. Either from me or some other means. I'll just have to deal with that when it happens."

"*We'll* just have to deal with it," she corrected. "You're not alone anymore. *We're* in this together."

Knowing that made him feel as if he was finally going to have the life he once imagined for himself, and he loved that it would include Nyla.

* * *

All things considered, Nyla was pleased at how the afternoon was going. She hadn't planned to introduce Harrison to her family yet, but he seemed to be enjoying himself. He was currently in the living room hanging out with her father, brother, and her nephew watching sports.

Lunch had been great, and though her mother hadn't embarrassed her too much, she still managed to ask Harrison how he felt about children. When he responded with—*I love kids and would like to have at least two*—Nyla was sure her mother fell in love with him.

"I thought you were lying about dating someone, and Harrison is gorgeous!" Dorian whisper shouted as they cleaned up the kitchen. Their mother, Essence, and Cree had disappeared to the B & B, leaving the two of them to take care of the dishes.

No way was Nyla going to admit to lying days ago, especially since her dating Harrison ended up not being a lie. Her problem was trying to act normal and not like some giddy teenager with a new boyfriend.

She told Dorian how they met and what a grump he'd been. Jamie had been right. It was fate that had brought her and Harrison together. What were the chances of her meeting the man of her dreams while working a temp job?

One story led to others, and before long, she and Dorian were laughing about the snowball fight. The more she shared, the more Nyla couldn't wait to make more fun memories with Harrison.

Cree strolled into the kitchen just as they finished loading the dishwasher and wiping down the counters.

"Dee, can you leave for a minute so I can talk to Nyla?"

Dorian glanced between the two of them. "Why? What's going on?"

Nyla wasn't sure either, but the seriousness in Cree's tone told her whatever her sister had to say, she wasn't going to like it.

"It's private, can you just give us a minute?" Cree said with more authority.

Dorian tossed the dish towel on the counter. "Fine, but Nyla's just going to tell me whatever you two talk about anyway."

The moment she left the room, Cree asked, "How well do you know Harrison Grant?"

Nyla knew immediately that her sister had figured out where she knew him from.

"I know him well enough," Nyla said firmly, looking at her sister and daring her to say the wrong thing.

Granted, part of Harrison's story could probably be found online, though Nyla hadn't checked. But she had no intention of discussing his personal life with anyone, not even her family. If he wanted to tell them anything, that was up to him. They wouldn't hear it from her.

Cree narrowed her eyes. "You know he spent time in prison for something he didn't do?"

"Yes," Nyla said firmly, hoping her sister would take the hint that this was not the time or place for this conversation.

"And you know *everything*?" Cree asked skeptically. "You know about his dysfunctional family, specifically his brother and mother?"

"Yes," Nyla ground out and crossed her arms over her chest, then tapped her foot impatiently, determined not to make this into a lengthy conversation.

Silence pulsed between them before her sister said, "Okay, I just wanted to make sure you knew who you were involved with."

"I know who Harrison is."

Cree nodded. "Good, and for the record, he seems like a nice guy. I wish you two well." With that, she turned and walked out as quietly as she'd entered.

Nyla released the breath she hadn't realized she'd been holding. They all would eventually know some portion of Harrison's story, but she had no doubt that they'd grow to care about him as much as she did.

"Oh good. You're alone," her mother said as she breezed into the kitchen with a sly smile on her face. "Let's talk weddings."

Nyla burst out laughing. "Mom! Let's not!"

Her mother laughed and wrapped her arms around Nyla. "I'm just kidding, honey. I'm glad you brought Harrison by.

He's a sweetheart. Make sure you bring him around often. I have a feeling he could benefit from our type of love."

"Aww, Mom." Nyla returned her hug, feeling an overwhelming sense of rightness. "You're the best, but I'll only agree to that if you promise not to hound us about grandkids."

Virginia tsked. "I'm not making any promises, but I'll try."

"That's all I ask. I love you, Mom."

"I love you too, honey."

Virginia Priestly might drive all of them nuts sometimes, but after hearing Harrison's story, Nyla loved and appreciated her mother even more. She was truly one of a kind.

Chapter Twenty-Two

Nyla parked her car in the parking deck of Gordon's lawyer's office and grinned like she'd just won a million bucks. Today, after she signed a few papers and ensured the transfer of funds went through, she'd finally be a business owner.

She was early for the appointment and sat back in her seat to stare out the windshield. The view was of another office building, but she barely noticed, since she was just glad to take a breather.

The past month had been a whirlwind of activity, but it had also been the best month she'd had in years. Not only did she finally have a dependable vehicle, but she also moved into a one-bedroom apartment not far from Moody Days. More importantly, she could afford both.

It had been hard not to accept Harrison's offer for her to move in with him. It would've been so easy, and she would've enjoyed them being under the same roof. But she was determined to start standing on her own. Besides, it was too soon for them to think about living together. Even if she was crazy in love with her man.

Joy bubbled up inside of her each time she thought about him. "I love Harrison Grant," she said into the quietness of the car. Neither of them had spoken those three little words—I love you—to one another, but they showed each other how they felt in so many other ways. Whether it was him making sure she always had gas in her car, or her sometimes having a nice dinner prepared for him when he got home from work.

It was the small gestures of thoughtfulness that added to their dating life. They might not have been together long, but Nyla was learning that it was about the quality of time they spent with each other. Not the length of time.

She and Harrison saw each other almost every day, and when they didn't, they called or texted. He was truly a gift from God, and she was grateful to have him in her life. There had been days when she'd been overwhelmed with all that she'd had going on, but a hug, a kiss, or just hearing his voice settled her down.

They were great together, and of course Jamie was taking all the credit. He claimed that he might start his own matchmaking business.

Nyla jumped when her phone alarm sounded, signaling she had ten minutes to get to the lawyer's office. She grabbed her bag and climbed out of the car, hoping that Cree was either already there or on her way.

Nyla would've preferred having Harrison by her side today, but they had agreed that since he was a silent investor, it would be better if he stayed away. Instead, Cree would be with her, which was good. It made sense to have legal counsel with her.

When Nyla entered the building, Cree was waiting near the information desk.

"Hey, sis. Thanks for coming," Nyla said as they shared a quick hug.

"Of course. I'm glad you asked me to come with you. I wouldn't have wanted you to sign any papers without a lawyer looking over them." As they rode the elevator to the fifth floor, Cree asked, "Are you ready for this?"

Nyla nodded, unable to hide her grin. "I'm more than ready. I was born to own a jazz club," she said and laughed.

Cree snickered. "I know I don't say it enough, but I'm really proud of you."

A warm glow flowed through Nyla at her sister's heartfelt words. "That means a lot coming from you. After your version of a pep talk months ago about how I needed to grow up," Nyla grinned when Cree groaned, "I had to agree. It was just the kick in the butt I needed to get myself together. So thanks for that."

Smiling, Cree wrapped her arm around Nyla's shoulder and pulled her close, giving her a little squeeze. "Anytime. That's what big sisters are for."

When they made it to the law office, Nyla was about to give her name to the receptionist, but they saw Gordon.

"We're in here," he said from down a short hall and pointed to an open door.

They followed him into a small conference room. After introductions, his lawyer went over the paperwork with them. Thirty minutes later, documents signed, and handshakes given, Nyla walked out as the new owner of Moody Days Jazz Club.

"I can't believe it," she squealed and threw her arms around her sister, laughing. "I did it!"

"Yes, you did, Ms. Business Owner. How are you planning to celebrate?" Cree asked as they headed to the elevator.

"I was thinking of closing the club one night and having a private party there just for family and close friends. I also thought that it could be a double celebration since Zion's thirtieth birthday is coming up."

"That's a great idea. Let me know if you need my help. Oh, and there's a reporter I know who would love to interview you about Moody Days. I figured you'd be interested because it'll be a way of getting some free advertisement."

"Yes! I'm definitely interested."

"Good, here's his card. Give him a call when you're ready to set something up."

Nyla practically floated to her car. She'd done it. She had saved, sacrificed, and made a lifelong dream into reality. Her dad always said, if you work hard, anything is possible, and she proved that to be true.

And this is only the beginning.

When she climbed into her car, instead of driving away, she pulled out her phone and called her favorite person. The phone rang several times before he picked up.

"Is this the new owner of Moody Days Jazz Club?" Harrison said by way of greeting, and Nyla laughed.

"As a matter of fact, it is!" She squealed and was grinning from ear to ear as if he could see her.

"Damn, baby, I'm so proud of you. I knew you could do it."

Nyla placed her hand over her heart, suddenly choked up. "I couldn't have done it without you." And she meant it. He trusted her enough to invest in her and her dream. That was something she would never forget.

"Yeah, you could've done it yourself. It might've taken a little longer, but that club would've been yours one day."

He was right. She'd been determined to own the club no matter what but having his financial support made it happen sooner.

"Harrison."

"Yeah?"

"Thank you for believing in me."

"Always, baby. I'll always believe in you."

* * *

Tonight was the night.

Nyla had been a ball of energy since early that morning in anticipation of the celebration tonight. She and Harrison had been busy coordinating contractors, overseeing every single detail of renovations she'd wanted to have done. They'd even helped with a few.

She had closed the club for two weeks. During that time, the minor makeover included a fresh coat of paint throughout the building, new shelving and mirrors behind the bar, and they'd updated the sound system.

Those small changes were just the beginning of her short-term plans for the club, and they had made a world of difference. Nyla couldn't wait for her family and friends to see the improvements. They'd all be there soon, and she had a few more tasks to take care of before her guests arrived.

First, she needed to finish up this interview with the reporter, Milton, who was sitting on the other side of the desk typing furiously on his tablet. He'd been there for an hour, and though he had asked great questions, he seemed to be jotting down every single word she said. Which was taking forever.

But she couldn't afford to complain. He worked for a local newspaper that had a ton of subscribers. No way would she pass up a free opportunity to spread the word about Moody Days.

"All right, Nyla, I think I have everything I need." Milton shoved his tablet into his messenger bag before standing. "Thanks again for your time, and thanks for the invite to the celebration tonight. I'm looking forward to it," he said as she walked him to the door.

"Good. I'll see you later."

She moved back to her desk, but before she could reclaim her seat, Harrison strolled in wearing his Black Knight Rider gear. The man looked like a big, strong, intimidating, badass. Nyla loved his Clark Kent daytime persona, but his musician disguise made her horny as hell. He was all broad shoulders, wide chest, and muscles everywhere she looked. And suddenly, she wanted him like a chocoholic wanted chocolate.

She rushed past him, slammed the door closed, and locked it before turning back to him. He had already shed his hat and coat and was now looking at her strangely.

"How about a quickie?" she said as she started stripping out of her clothes.

Harrison stood in the middle of the room, his eyes suddenly like hot molten lava as he watched her undress. Nyla was already wet for him, but when his tongue snaked out and swiped his bottom lip, she grew wetter. When all her clothes sat in a pile on the floor, she ran and leaped into his arms, knowing he'd catch her.

Sputtering, it was like his shock had stolen his words until he said, "Whoa, babe! Hello to you too." His deep baritone was huskier than usual. "Though I love seeing you naked, but here? What's gotten into you?"

"Hopefully, you in like sixty seconds if we're going to get in a quickie, and I mean it has to be super quick because people will be here soon," she said while grinding against him as she nuzzled his neck.

Harrison held her tighter, moaning as she started sucking on his neck. Then his erotic sounds turned into a curse when he stumbled back, bumping into the desk.

"Okay. Okay wait," he said in a rush and suddenly set her on her feet.

At first, Nyla started to protest as she squeezed her thighs together, struggling to tamp down the delicious ache between her legs. But then Harrison wasted no time getting out of his boots, jeans, and his boxer briefs. He didn't even bother with his shirt. Instead, he dug for his wallet and removed a condom.

After making quick work of sheathing himself, he hauled her into his arms again and backed her to a nearby wall.

"I didn't know you could move that fast," she said, breathing hard as if she'd just sprinted a mile. And before Nyla could form her next thought, Harrison drove into her in one smooth move, and she cried out in pleasure as her inner muscles adjusted to his thick shaft.

Harrison's fingers dug into the back of her thighs while he drove into her like a man possessed, and Nyla held on for the ride.

Just seeing him walk through the door had her wet with need. It wouldn't take long for her to reach her release, especially with how good he felt buried deep inside of her. She was already teetering on the edge.

"Ba—baby," Harrison ground out as his thrusts grew more frantic. "Come for me. I need you to... Ahhh sh..."

Nyla lost it. She cried out as her body tightened around him, and her release hurtled through her hard and powerful. Harrison was right behind her, holding her closer as his growl shattered the quietness in the room. Then he nailed her to the wall with his hard body.

"*Oh, my goodness,*" Nyla wheezed, her nails still digging into his shoulders, while she felt as if she'd just ridden a roller coaster.

"Damn, baby," Harrison heaved, his breath warm against her neck. "Feel free to...to greet me like that all the time. What the hell did that reporter ask you to get you all hot and ready for me?"

Nyla snorted a laugh. "It—it had nothing to do… with him," she said, still panting. "It was all you, babe. You and your sexy Knight Rider gear."

"Noted," he said, then eventually lowered her body until her feet touched the floor. "We're doing this again, but slower when I take you home. Right now, though, we need to hurry and get cleaned up."

Chapter Twenty-Three

"That was *hot*," Nyla said a short while later, her body still humming with pleasure. They were back in her office, refreshed and dressed just in time to get the party started.

"I agree. That was incredible, and so are you. You look hella good, by the way," Harrison said, his heated gaze eating her up. "I'm digging the outfit. Is that what you're performing in tonight?" he asked, moving to sit on the edge of the desk. Nyla glanced down at her clothes.

Like him, she was wearing all black. That included a long-sleeve T-shirt, baggy cargo pants that hung low on her hips, and even combat boots that Harrison had bought for her a couple of weeks ago. Even her fingernails were black. Her jewelry, a bulky chain-link necklace and a long chain-link belt around her waist, were thick and bold.

"Yeah, since we'll be on stage together, I figured I'd try to blend in with the Black Knight's attire."

Harrison nodded, smiling approvingly at her. "You look sexy. I'm looking forward to performing with you tonight. I was thinking maybe we can start with John Legend's 'Ordinary People' before we roll into Pharell's 'Happy.'"

"Sounds good. Maybe you can play your bass for those and then switch to your sax for Marvin Gaye's 'What's Going on.' I'd like that one to be all instrumental if you're okay with that."

"Works for me."

It had been his idea for them to perform together on stage, and Nyla agreed. From the moment they started dating, they'd been spending a lot of time in his music room. Her favorite room in his house. She had never dated a musician before, and she was glad Harrison was her first. They literally made beautiful music together.

He would be the main entertainer for the night, and then a DJ would take over.

"Hey you guys," Jamie said from the opened office door. "I hope you're ready to get this night started. The caterers are all set up, and your parents just arrived. Your mom wants to know if you need help with anything. Do you want me to send them back, or are you coming out here?" he asked Nyla.

"No, tell her she's a guest tonight, and I'll be right out."

"Will do. See you guys out there."

"Are you ready for tonight?" she asked Harrison.

"I should be asking you that. Your family and friends will be here, and you'll be playing hostess all night. Can you handle it?"

When he stood, she looped her arm through his, and they headed for the door. "As long as you're nearby, I can handle anything. Let's do this."

Hours later, Harrison pulled Nyla to the dance floor just as the DJ played Roxette's, "It Must've Been Love."

"I've been wanting to dance with the prettiest woman in the club all night," he said, holding her snug against his hard body as they began to sway to the music. "You doing okay?"

"I'm great, Mr. Sweet-talker." She smiled up at him, then squeaked when he spun her before pulling her back into his arms. Laughing, she touched her lips to his. "I love dancing with you."

She still remembered the first time they danced together. It was the first night at her apartment, and they were in her small kitchen unpacking pots and pans that she'd had in storage. Music was playing, as usual, and Eric Benét's "Spend Your Life With Me" poured through the speaker. After their dance, Harrison insisted that was their song.

Even in their short time together, Nyla had a list of special memories like that one.

"Sometimes it's hard to remember what my life was like before you came along," she said close to his ear. "I just..." She started to say more but instead leaned her head back and stared into his intense brown eyes.

"I love you," he said, surprising her. "I love you so damn much, and I don't want to think about how empty my life was before you came along."

A huge smile kicked up the corners of her mouth, and her heart overflowed with love for this man. "I love you, too, sweetheart. A lot!"

He laughed and captured her mouth with his as if sealing their revelation with a kiss.

Nyla's heart thundered. There was a dreamy intimacy with this kiss, and she savored every tender lap of his tongue. It didn't matter they were opposites in so many ways. There were times like this she was reminded of how perfect they were together.

"Excuse me. May I cut in?"

Nyla pulled her mouth from Harrison's, and she burst out laughing when she realized it was her mother doing the asking.

"Really, Mom?" Nyla said, grinning. "Can't you dance with Dad or *anybody* else?"

Her mother planted a hand on her hip. "Your dad is tired of dancing, and I can't find Zion. He's probably hiding or something. Besides, I want to dance with the newest member of our family. You don't mind, do you, Harrison?"

Harrison let out a full belly laugh, which made Nyla start laughing. "Mrs. Priestly, it would be a pleasure to dance with you. *You don't mind do you, Nyla?*" he said, his lips twitching as if he was trying not to laugh again.

Nyla sighed playfully. "*Fine.* I guess I can find something else to do."

As she left them on the dance floor, Nyla was pretty sure she fell a little more in love with her man in that moment. She slowly made her way to the bar, weaving around groups of people and tables, glad to see everyone enjoying themselves.

She thought about how her mother had been pulling Harrison into their family little by little, and if she wasn't mistaken, Virginia Priestly was growing on Harrison too. It was fun to watch him get flustered when she'd say or do something that embarrassed him.

Like the other day when they were at the B & B, and her mom asked Harrison if he would escort her to her church's annual banquet in a few weeks. Nyla's dad couldn't attend, and Zion had outright said *no*. Then her mom's attention went to Harrison, and everyone cracked up when he agreed to attend.

He was going to regret it later, which was why the family had been laughing. Virginia liked to be the first person to arrive at events and was often the last one to leave. In between that time, she insisted on talking to everyone, and there was no doubt she'd want Harrison by her side the whole time.

With him spending time around her mom, Nyla hoped he'd one day want to see his mother. She wasn't sure what that would look like, but getting some type of closure, where she was concerned, would be good for him.

Nyla went to the bar. "Hey, Jamie, can I have a bottle of water?"

"Sure thing, *Boss Lady*."

She smiled at his term of endearment while he opened the bottle and handed it to her. "Thanks, and thanks for being here. I still think you should've been a guest instead of insisting on working the bar."

"I know, but you know I love bartending. Besides, Dre needed to attend his daughter's recital," he said of their only other bartender.

Hiring another bartender was on the top of Nyla's list of things to do. She also needed a couple of more servers. Her to-do list was growing by the day, but she was too excited about being her own boss to care.

"You did good, sis," Zion said, sidling up to her while taking a sip of what looked to be whiskey in his glass. "This place looks great and speaking of great, you and Harrison on stage sounded sensational together. Good enough to take your act on the road. If you guys decide to do that, let me know. I'll be your bodyguard."

When he started flexing his biceps through the fitted Henley he wore, Nyla couldn't help but laugh.

"I'll keep that in mind. So what, no date tonight? I thought for sure you'd be strolling in here with a woman on each arm. It's your birthday. You're slipping."

He snorted and shook his head. "Nah, I didn't need to bring anyone. I figured there'd be enough women here for me to choose from."

"Yeah, right. You didn't bring anyone because everyone probably turned you down," she joked.

They both laughed, knowing she was full of it. That was

one thing her brother never had a problem with—picking up women. He was a good-looking man, and he knew it. She had witnessed him catching the eye of plenty of ladies of all ages over the years, and he didn't hesitate to pour on the charm.

But lately, he seemed to have settled down some. Now that Nyla thought about it, Zion had been flying solo more often than not.

"Are you dating someone?" she asked, wondering if he was keeping a woman out of sight for fear their mother would start hounding him for grandkids.

He narrowed his eyes at her. "Why? Are you turning into Mom and planning to try to fix me up with someone?"

"No way. I can't stand it when she does it to me. So, you don't have to worry about me doing it to you."

After a long hesitation, he said, "Between you and me, I met someone almost a year ago while I was attending a conference. She wasn't one of the attendees, but she'd been at the hotel bar one night, and we hit it off. Problem is my dating life hasn't been the same since. I keep comparing everybody to her."

"*Really?* Does that mean you found *the one?* And when are we going to meet her?"

"Well, that's the thing. I don't know how to get in contact with her. I only hung out with her that *one* night and..."

Nyla gasped playfully, bringing her hand to her mouth as if she were in shock. "Don't tell me you had a one-night stand," she whispered.

Harrison rolled his eyes skyward. "Don't be weird. Despite what you and our sisters think, I'm a grown man."

Nyla laughed. "If you say so, but what are you going to do about your mystery lady? You're a cop. Can't you use your cop skills and hunt her down?"

He shook his head. "I don't know her last name. Hell, I'm

not even sure she gave me her real first name. Besides, the conference was in Vegas. She could live anywhere."

"Ahhh," was all Nyla could say, and before she could think of anything encouraging to say, a beautiful woman approached the bar, asking if he wanted to dance.

"Duty calls," Zion said to Nyla and handed her his empty glass before taking the woman's hand and leading her to the dance floor.

She had just set the glass on the bar when Harrison's strong arms wrapped around her. He placed a kiss against her neck before she turned and faced him.

"Hey you," she said and gave him a quick peck on the lips.

"Hi." He looped his arm around her shoulders. "It looks like the party is a success. Not that I'm surprised," he said as they stared out at the crowd.

"I agree, and thanks for all your help. I know I keep saying this...about almost everything lately, but I couldn't have done this without you."

He kissed her, and Nyla felt more content than she'd felt in a very long time.

My own business. Wonderful, supportive family. A sexy, smart, loving man. My life is perfect.

Chapter Twenty-Four

Harrison stood in the middle of his new office and glanced around. He'd had a lot of changes in his life over the last few months, and he was embracing every single one. Change was good. That wasn't always how he felt, especially during the times he'd wanted to stay in the shadows, keep his head down, and pretend his life wasn't as bad as it seemed.

Those days were over. He was looking forward to his new role at Telecom. Looking forward to his life with Nyla, and he was looking forward to his future.

"Well, I guess it's official. You're the big boss now," Royce said from behind him, and Harrison turned toward the door.

He owed this man so much. Royce had almost single-handedly saved his life in almost every way possible. How was he ever going to be able to thank the guy? The words *thank you* didn't seem to be enough to express how much he appreciated him.

Royce lifted his hands and shook his head. "I know that

look. Before you start thanking me for something, save it." He moved farther into the office and closed the door. "Even though my brothers helped get this business off the ground, you've been my right-hand man since then. There's no way we could've turned this into a million-dollar company without your help. You're like a brother to me. You don't owe me anything, in case that's what you were thinking."

Harrison chuckled and rubbed the back of his neck. "I forget how well you know me." He and Royce shook hands and pulled each other in for a man hug, back pounding and all. "I feel the same about you. I know you don't want to hear it, and I promise this will be the last time, but thank you for standing by me all those years ago. You'll never understand how much it meant to have you believe in me. Someone to stand for me when I couldn't stand for myself. I appreciate you man."

Harrison gave him another hug before stepping back.

"Like my grandfather often says, just pay it forward. None of us can survive in this world alone, and occasionally we all need a helping hand. Just be there for the next person who might need someone to support them in their darkest days."

Harrison nodded.

"I will, and your grandfather sounds like a wise man."

"He's the best man I know. You'll have to come to Cincinnati for a visit, and I'll introduce you to the great Steven Jenkins," he said with pride.

"I'll do that, and I'll make sure I'm there on a Sunday so I can get in on your grandmother's Sunday brunch."

Royce laughed. "Yeah man. You have never had good eating until you've tasted my grandmother's cooking."

The way Royce talked about how every weekend the Jenkins family put on a feast and came together to eat sounded like an event more than a brunch. Harrison had every intention of visiting one day, and hopefully Nyla would go with him.

Believing in You

His heart squeezed just thinking about her. They spent practically every day together, and Harrison couldn't imagine not having her in every aspect of his life going forward. It was too early to be thinking about marriage, but his ultimate goal was to one day marry Nyla and have a family.

He and Royce talked for a few minutes longer before Royce had to leave to catch a plane. Harrison had just sat at his new desk, prepared to get some work done, when his cell phone buzzed.

A smile found his lips because he assumed it was Nyla. They were having lunch soon, and she should be there any minute. But when he glanced at the screen, it was a text from Veronica.

I'm surprised you agreed to an interview.

"What?" he mumbled before he clicked on the attached link.

Wrongly Accused Murderer Returns to Society

"What the actual hell?"

His pulse pounded loudly in his ears as he started reading the article. Shock and anger warred within him, and he gripped his phone hard enough to split it into two. He glanced at the name of the reporter, and his fury spiked. It was the guy who had interviewed Nyla about her being the new owner of Moody Days and the changes in store.

But instead of reporting about the jazz club, the write-up included his story, details that he'd shared with Nyla months ago. It even mentioned how his mother chose to protect Geoffrey over him.

"Dammit!" he ground out, as he continued reading his life in black and white. How could Nyla have gone behind his back like this?

A knock sounded on his opened door, and Harrison lifted his gaze. Nyla stood there smiling and holding a large picnic basket. He wasn't sure what she saw on his face, but her smile dropped, and worry replaced it.

"What's wrong?" she asked and hurried into the office.

"Close the door," Harrison demanded gruffer than intended, but he couldn't believe her reporter friend or whoever the hell the guy had been could print such trash.

"I trusted you with my deepest, darkest secret. The most *humiliating* thing that's ever happened to me, and what did you do?" He held up his phone. "You shared the story with some damn reporter!"

"Harrison, I have no idea what you're talking about, but clearly, you're upset. But what you're not going to do is yell at me and talk to me any kind of way," she said, her voice low but a little shaky as she set the basket on the table. "Maybe you should tell me exactly what you're accusing me of."

Without a word, he shoved his phone at her. While she read, he paced behind his desk as his chest heaved. He didn't stop moving until he heard Nyla gasp, and he turned to her. She was still reading and gripping the phone as hard as he'd done moments ago.

He released a ragged breath and placed his palms on the desk. Maybe he'd overreacted. He hadn't even read the whole article, but seeing the name of the reporter and reading what he had before Nyla came in, had him immediately thinking the worst.

Nyla wasn't Veronica or his mother. She wouldn't intentionally hurt him. He knew that on a certain level. Yet, there was a part of him so used to the women in his life betraying him that it was easy to forget everyone wasn't like them.

"Who is Karen Bouchard? The reporter quoted her a few times," Nyla said, her head still down as she continued reading.

Unease clawed through Harrison before he said, "She was Geoffrey's girlfriend. She's the one who lied, giving

Geoffrey an alibi for where he was at the time of the murder."

Karen had eventually been charged with perjury and obstruction but cut a deal with the prosecutor and got her sentence reduced. She served a year in prison, received several years of probation, and was charged a hefty fine that she was probably still trying to pay.

Harrison had no idea what she was doing these days. Except, apparently, she was talking to reporters.

"Was anything in the article a lie?" Nyla asked, setting his cell phone on the desk.

Harrison ran his hands down his face, feeling like a complete jerk for the way he'd talked to her. "Not the parts I read. You came in when I got to the section about me getting arrested at work and dumped by my fiancée." He moved around the desk. "I'm sorry, baby. I overreacted when I accused you of—"

Nyla placed her finger over his lips, and he stopped talking. Thankfully, she didn't look like she wanted to murder him, but he couldn't miss the disappointment in her pretty brown eyes. God, he hoped she wasn't going to break up with him, but unlike with Veronica, he would fight for Nyla.

"You're lucky I'm in love with you," she said. "Otherwise, I would knock you upside your head with my purse."

His lips twitched under her finger, but he didn't allow himself to smile. It was clear he'd hurt her even though she sounded calm. He saw the disappointment in her eyes.

"I would never betray you in any way. Don't you know that by now?" she asked, her words cutting him deeply as she dropped her hand from his mouth. "I know it was a shock seeing your story in that article, but you must know I'm on your side, Harrison. I always will be, and I want you happy, healthy, and... I want the best for you. Don't you know that?"

He lunged forward and wrapped her in his arms. "I do. I know. I messed up. I reacted before thinking, and I'm so sorry for accusing you. Not only was I wrong to do that, but it's past time I get over this shit."

Nyla didn't relax in his arms until he spoke those last words.

"Yes, it is," she said and leaned her head back to look up at him. "For the record, I haven't told anyone your story and I never will. It's your story to tell. The only thing the reporter and I discussed was Moody Days. Maybe since he stayed for the party and heard you playing, he thought you would make for a more interesting story. I don't know, but you better believe he's going to hear from me.

"But getting back to you. What you went through was horrible. No one should have to go through something like that, and I know you were humiliated." She fisted the front of his button-down shirt. "I don't want to sound insensitive, but we've all been humiliated at one time or another. It's a part of life. We can let it fester inside of us, or we can move past it. This." She waved her hand at the phone on the desk. "You going off whenever you see something written about you, or hear someone talking about your past, can't keep happening."

Harrison nodded and reached for her hand. "I agree. It stops right now, but do you forgive me?"

"Of course I do," she said and kissed him. "*I love you, man.*"

"And I love you." He cupped her face between his hands. "I love you so damn much it scares me sometimes. I also trust you more than I thought I could ever trust another human being. I never want to hurt you or disappoint you. You mean everything to me. I'm so sorry."

"I know," she said before kissing him deeply.

They were going to be okay. He was going to make sure of

that because he was looking forward to all the wonderful things the future had in store for them.

Epilogue

Harrison stood with Nyla outside of his sister's apartment building, almost ready to do something he thought he'd never do. See his mother. When Piper called a few days ago, asking if he'd reconsider seeing their mother, Harrison had conceded. Shocking him and her. He'd been thinking about doing it for a while now, and he thought he was ready.

Now he wasn't so sure.

His sister, the peacemaker, wanted them all to be a family again. Harrison couldn't promise that, but he really wanted to close this chapter of his life. A chapter riddled with hurt and disappointment.

"You're not changing your mind, are you?" Nyla asked, her fingers interlocked with his.

She looked sexy in a long, black coat and a short black-and-white checkered dress that stopped just above her knees. She had paired the outfit with a pair of thigh-high boots that had chunky heels and silver chains around the ankles.

Of course, she still wore rings on every finger and silver

bangles on her wrists because she said her outfits are incomplete without them. Though she hadn't totally moved away from her grunge look, she'd been dressing up more. She called her new style sophisticated grunge. He honestly didn't care what she wore, she was still the most beautiful woman to him.

"Have you?" she prompted.

"No, but let's go in there before I do change my mind."

A short while later, he knocked on the door.

"It's going to be okay," Nyla whispered and gave his hand a slight squeeze.

He was sure he wouldn't have been able to do this without having her by his side. She often told him that he was her rock, but he felt it was the other way around. The unwavering support she'd been giving him the last couple of months as he got acclimated to his new position at Telecom, had been everything he needed and more.

The apartment door opened suddenly, and Piper ran out and practically knocked Harrison over with her hug. He laughed, marveled at how good it felt to see her. It had been a couple of months since they'd been face-to-face, though they talked often.

His sister had always been a girlie girl, and her appearance reflected that. Her hair hung in loose waves around her shoulder, and her attire consisted of a light-pink blouse paired with off-white pants and pink flats.

"I thought for sure you'd cancel, but I'm so glad you didn't," she said and then turned her attention to Nyla. She greeted her the same way, with a hearty hug. "Hey, Nyla! I'm so glad we're finally meeting. It's nice to put a face with a voice, and girl, I'm loving the outfit. *Nice.*"

"Thank you," Nyla said. "And it's great to finally meet you too."

"Okay. I'm sorry. I guess I should've at least let you guys

inside before attacking," Piper said on a laugh and ushered them into the spacious apartment.

Harrison had been there often, but his sister had made a few changes since the last time. Instead of white, the walls were painted a blue-gray, and she had also gotten new carpet that was a navy blue. Everything else, furniture, cabinets, and a few accessories were white. Anyone could tell she didn't have kids or pets.

"You guys have a seat. Mom is in the bathroom. Can I get you something to drink?"

Before he and Nyla could respond, Harrison's mother came into view.

His heart rate kicked up as they stared across the room at each other. She looked different from the last time he'd seen her. She used to have long, thick hair that went down her back, and for the most part, that was the same. Except now, there was more gray than black, and her hair hung in loose curls around her shoulders.

She'd lost weight. The sallowness of her face and the dark circles under her eyes looked like a person who was ill and didn't sleep much. Two things that hadn't changed—she still wore berry red lipstick, and her nails were polished in the same color.

"Hi, Mom," he said, his voice shaking a little, but it didn't crack.

"*Harrison.*" That one word sounded like a whisper being carried away by a gust of wind.

Suddenly, tears streamed down her face, and she placed her hands over her mouth just as a sob broke free. His mother's cries, filled with so much anguish, was like being stabbed in the chest with a machete repeatedly.

Damn. He hadn't been prepared for this. But when Nyla squeezed his hand and discreetly gestured for him to go to his

Believing in You

mother, Harrison did. His legs were heavy, like they were covered in cement, as he moved across the room. When he was close to his mother, he gathered her into his arms and hugged her.

Months ago, he wouldn't have been able to do this. He wouldn't have been able to just hold her as she cried harder and louder while her body shook uncontrollably. But he was doing it, and surprisingly enough, he had Virginia Priestly to thank for this ability.

Mrs. Priestly greeted him with warm, gentle, *I-love-you-to-death* type hugs every time she saw him, and she didn't allow him to leave her presence without giving him another one. He felt each one to the depths of his soul. Every. Single. Time.

Now it was his turn to give one to his mother.

No, they could never have a normal relationship, but he could give her something that he never thought he'd ever be able to give her—forgiveness.

"I forgive you," he said quietly next to her ear, and she cried harder. Her arms tightened around him, and she held on as if he was a lifeline that she had no intention of ever letting go.

Harrison didn't know how long they stood like that, but by the time they released each other, it was as if a boulder had lifted from his shoulders. *Finally.* Even without a lot of words or a lengthy, heated conversation, he could close this chapter of his past.

Two hours after arriving, they left Piper's apartment and Nyla was emotionally spent. She didn't know what she expected from the visit, but all things considered, it went well.

As she and Harrison walked silently hand in hand down the two flights of stairs, she thought about the conversation that took place in the apartment. Nicole Grant, Harrison's mother, was a lovely woman who was weighed down heavily with sorrow and guilt.

The reason she had been calling Harrison lately was because she'd had a health scare. After being rushed to the hospital weeks ago, thinking she'd had a heart attack, it turned out to be angina. Still, it gave her the push she needed to try to talk to Harrison. She wanted to ask his forgiveness before she took her last breath.

Though Harrison had forgiven her, without her having to say a word, Mrs. Grant still begged him for forgiveness. It took awhile for the conversation to take off, but she initiated it by apologizing to him over and over again. She told him that there was no excuse for her behavior back then. That there was nothing she could say now, not even *I'm sorry*, that could ever make up for the horrible decisions she'd made when he'd been accused of murder.

Nyla felt the woman's pain and anguish deep in her soul. Every word and every tear held so much sorrow and guilt. Harrison told his mother that he wasn't there to rehash what took place years ago. He was there for both of them to get closure and to heal from the experience.

Even though Nyla believed Harrison truly forgave his mother, she wondered if his mother would ever forgive herself. Nyla didn't know what would become of their family's relationship. Yet, she hoped this visit opened the door for future visits, and all of them would start the healing process and one day grow closer.

The moment they stepped outside into the spring air, Nyla sucked in a breath and released it slowly. It wasn't very warm out, but at least the sun was shining, and the wind was mild.

As they walked down the block to where Harrison had parked, he didn't speak until he reached the SUV. Instead of opening the passenger door, he backed Nyla up against the vehicle and stood in front of her.

"I'll never be able to thank you enough for coming here with me today. I know for a fact that I couldn't have done this without you and your mother."

Nyla frowned. "*My* mother?"

He nodded, and a slow smile spread across his face. "She taught me how to hug."

Nyla laughed. She didn't have to ask him what that meant, she knew. Her mother gave the best hugs. It was almost like her hugs had a silent conversation built into them that spoke of love, trust, and probably in Harrison's case, forgiveness.

"I'm so proud of you," Nyla said, sliding her hands up his chest until her arms circled his neck. "I knew you could do this."

"I'm glad I came. It feels like a heavy weight has been lifted off my shoulders. Thanks for believing that I could do this. Your support meant everything."

"I'll always believe in you," she said and kissed him slowly. When the kiss ended, Harrison was smiling. "What?" she asked.

"Nothing. I was thinking about how much I love you. I think I might've fallen in love with you that day at Telecom when you offered me tequila at nine o'clock in the morning."

Nyla threw her head back and laughed. "I love you, too, even when you're grumpy, and I have to offer you liquor to calm you down."

Harrison chuckled and wrapped his strong arms around her. When he placed a lingering kiss on the side of her head, Nyla closed her eyes and basked in his love.

* * *

Sneak Peek – Zion's story...

Zion Priestly entered his parents' bed and breakfast and stopped short when he saw his mother holding an infant.

"Mom, please tell me you didn't steal someone's baby."

He was only half joking. She'd been on a mission, insisting he and his sisters get married and give her grandbabies. It started when they all reached their mid-twenties, and no one seemed to be in a hurry to settle down and have kids.

Zion had recently turned thirty. He had barely blown out the candles on the birthday cake that she had baked before asking if he was dating anyone. That was code for—do you have a potential baby momma lined up yet?

Getting married and having children were the last things on his mind. As a Chicago police officer, his workdays were long and exhausting. Some days he barely had the energy to drag his tired body home after a shift. Going home and having to fulfill husband and daddy duties? *No thank you.*

"Well, since my own kids won't give me more grandkids, I'm forced to borrow babies," his mother said, pulling him out of his thoughts.

Zion chuckled. "You're a trip," he said and kissed his mother's cheek. In doing so, he glanced at the gorgeous baby girl with big light-brown eyes, a tiny nose, and bow-shaped lips. She was dressed in all pink and had to be the prettiest baby he'd ever seen. "She's a cutie-pie."

Unable to help himself, he smiled at the little one and touched her tiny hand while quietly baby-talking to her. When the baby offered him a smile, his heart nearly stopped.

"See, you're a natural," his mother said. "All you have to do is find a wife and start having a few cutie-pies like this one. Don't you want to hold her?"

He shook his head. "Mom, don't start."

Zion took a step back but couldn't take his gaze from the baby. If he wasn't in his police uniform, he'd consider holding her for a minute. He loved kids, especially when they belonged to someone else.

"Okay, Mrs. Priestly. Thank you so much for entertaining her while I fixed a bottle. I…"

The stunning woman stopped talking and gazed at Zion. When she did, shock roiled inside of him, and his pulse thumped double-time.

It's her.

He'd recognize those gorgeous eyes anywhere. It was the woman he had met in Vegas during a conference almost a year ago. He hadn't been able to stop thinking about her, and now she was standing only a couple of feet away.

Her mouth dropped open, and if it was possible, her eyes grew as large as dinner plates.

"*You,*" she whispered.

Coming Spring 2025
***

If you enjoyed this story, please consider leaving a review on review sites or social media outlets.

Dear Reader

Dear Reader,
Hopefully you enjoyed Harrison and Nyla's story, as well as the introduction to the Priestly Family series! They are a fun group of characters who I can't wait for you to meet on a more intimate level—starting with Zion and his mystery lady. Hopefully, you enjoyed the little tease from their story which will be released Spring 2025.

Also, for you fans of the Jenkins & Sons Construction series, did you catch a few hints that I dropped in? One being— Royce (Jenkins) Garrison. Many of you will remember that Royce was first introduced in UNPLANNED LOVE. Though he's loved by the majority of the Jenkins family, he and his cousin Liam Jenkins still have an unresolved issue. Let's just say there are more cousins and more stories to come! Stay tuned...

In the meantime, if you're not currently a subscriber to my newsletter, now is a great time to sign up! It's the best way to get sneak peeks into upcoming stories, and you'll find out about new releases before anyone else. You'll also hear about giveaways that are exclusive to my newsletter subscribers. So go ahead, sign up!

https://sharoncooper.net/newsletter

Other Titles By Sharon

Atlanta's Finest Series
Vindicated (book 1)
Indebted (book 2)
Accused (book 3)
Betrayed (book 4)
Hunted (book 5)
Tempted (book 6)
Committed (book 7)
Protected (book 8)

Jenkins & Sons Construction Series (Contemporary Romance)
Love Under Contract (book 1)
Proposal for Love (book 2)
A Lesson on Love (book 3)
Unplanned Love (book 4)
Bid on Love (book 5)
The Cost of Love (book 6)

Jenkins Family Series (Contemporary Romance)
Best Woman for the Job (Short Story Prequel)
Still the Best Woman for the Job (book 1)
All You'll Ever Need (book 2)
Tempting the Artist (book 3)
Negotiating for Love (book 4)
Seducing the Boss Lady (book 5)
Love at Last (Holiday Novella)
When Love Calls (Novella)
More Than Love (Novella)

Reunited Series (Romantic Suspense)
Blue Roses (book 1)
Secret Rendezvous (Prequel to Rendezvous with Danger)
Rendezvous with Danger (book 2)
Truth or Consequences (book 3)
Operation Midnight (book 4)
Casino Heat (book 5)

Finding Love Series
Legal Seduction (Contemporary Romance)
A Dose of Passion (Contemporary Romance)
Model Attraction (Contemporary Romance)

Stand Alones
Something New ("Edgy" Sweet Romance)
Sin City Temptation (Contemporary Romance)
A Passionate Kiss (Contemporary Romance)
Soul's Desire (Unparalleled Love series)
Show Me (Irresistible Husband series)
His to Protect (Harlequin Romantic Suspense)

Sharon C. Cooper

His to Defend (Harlequin Romantic Suspense)
Business Not As Usual (Romantic Comedy)
In It to Win It (Romantic Comedy)
Kiss Me (Irresistible Husband – Contemporary Romance)
Mr. One and Only (Baes of Juneteenth)
Fiancé for Hire (Men for Hire)

About the Author

USA Today bestselling author Sharon C. Cooper loves anything involving romance with a happily-ever-after, whether in books, movies, or real life. She writes contemporary romance, romantic suspense, as well as romantic comedy. She enjoys rainy days, carpet picnics, and family game night. Her stories have won numerous awards, including The Rochelle Alers Best Series award for her Atlanta's Finest Series (2022) and The Beverly Jenkins Author of the Year award (2021). When she isn't writing, Sharon loves hanging out with her amazing husband, doing volunteer work, or reading a good book (a romance of course). To read more about Sharon and her novels, or to sign up to be notified of her latest releases, visit www.sharoncooper.net

www.ingramcontent.com/pod-product-compliance
Lightning Source LLC
Chambersburg PA
CBHW020953310525
27534CB00009B/335